Amazing Facts about
Australia

Author: Karin Cox

Principal Photographer: Steve Parish

Contents

Amazing **Australia**

the **FACTS!**

AUSTRALIA'S FLAG (above) was officially recognised in 1951, when King George VI approved the Australian Blue Ensign with the seven-pointed Commonwealth star beneath and the five-pointed Southern Cross constellation. In 1953, the *Flags Act* made it Australia's official flag. Australia has two other flags: the Aboriginal flag and the Torres Strait Islander flag, which were officially adopted on 14 July 1995. Each State and Territory also has its own flag.

THE COAT OF ARMS (below) consists of a shield bearing the badges of the six federated States. It is carried by a kangaroo and Emu (both animals that cannot go backwards — for good luck), which stand on an ornamental rest surrounded by wattle.

AUSTRALIA IS ABOUT the same size as the combined mainland States of the USA (except Alaska) and is approximately 32 times the size of the UK.

GREEN AND GOLD are the country's national colours and feature in the uniforms of national sports teams.

OPAL (right) is the country's national gemstone and Australia produces 97% of the world's supply. Some Aborigines call it "fire of the desert" and believe it is a gift from the sky.

Australia is simultaneously the world's smallest continent and the largest island on Earth. It was also, apart from Antarctica, one of the last land masses to be explored and settled by European people, with a European history of little more than 220 years. However, the Aboriginal history of Australia stretches back more than 60,000 years and is the oldest continuing culture on the planet.

THE AUSTRALIAN CONTINENT has an area of 7,682,300 km^2 and is comprised of two land masses — the mainland and Tasmania, as well as more than 8220 smaller islands, giving it a combined coastline of around 59,736 km. It lies on the Tropic of Capricorn and is surrounded by water — to the east by the Pacific Ocean and to the west by the Indian Ocean, with the Arafura Sea to the north and the Southern Ocean to the south. Australia is extremely remote, its closest neighbour is Papua New Guinea, which is around 200 km to the north. A number of external territories, such as Norfolk Island, the Cocos (Keeling) Islands, Christmas Island, Macquarie Island and the Australian Antarctic Territory (which lies between 45 degrees south and 160 degrees east), are also part of Australia.

DRIEST, FLATTEST, OLDEST

After Antarctica, Australia is the driest continent on Earth. Although the climate varies in different parts of the country, most of the inland is vast desert that is not suitable for human habitation. Because of Australia's strong sunshine and desert winds, 89% of the country's rainfall evaporates. In comparison, Europe and Africa average 60% evaporation and North America just 48%.

Around 250 million years of erosion have led to Australia becoming the flattest continent on Earth. The lowest mainland point is Lake Eyre, which is 16 m below sea level, and the highest is Mount Kosciuszko in New South Wales, which is 2228 m above sea level — still much lower than mountains found on other continents. Because Australia is so old and does not lie along any major underground fault lines, it is also the most stable land mass, and no mountain building events have occurred for the past 80 million years.

Above: The nation's floral emblem is the Golden Wattle (*Acacia pycnantha*).

Below: Australia's iconic kangaroo is the faunal emblem. Australia has three kangaroo species, the Eastern Grey, Western Grey and Red Kangaroo, as well as numerous smaller wallaby, wallaroo and potoroo species.

Above, left to right: Wallaman Falls in Lumholtz National Park, Qld, is the longest single-drop waterfall and plunges 305 m into a large pool; The Simpson Desert is home to the longest parallel sand dunes in the world, including the 40-m-high "Big Red"; Australia's longest river system, the Murray–Darling, nourishes the continent's south-eastern corner; Snow falls in Kosciuszko NP.

LAND BEFORE TIME

Because Australia is such an ancient, seemingly timeless place, many people have called it the "land before time". Certainly, the Aboriginal concept of time — in which the Dreaming (or world of the creation spirits) is ever-present and ongoing, including the past, present and future — makes that an apt title. However, Europeans brought with them their concept of time and today three different time zones operate across the vast continent. Queensland, New South Wales, Tasmania, Victoria and the Australian Capital Territory are half an hour ahead of South Australia and the Northern Territory, and two hours ahead of Western Australia. From October to April, New South Wales, Victoria, Tasmania and the Australian Capital Territory have daylight saving, advancing the clock an hour to enjoy more sunshine in the evening. The remaining states and territories — Queensland, the Northern Territory and Western Australia — do not observe daylight saving.

"DISCOVERING" A CONTINENT

Many people mistakenly believe that English Lieutenant (later Captain) James Cook (left) discovered Australia in 1770, but that is not the case. The first known discoverers were the ancestors of Aboriginal or Torres Strait Islander people, who (as some DNA evidence suggests) crossed by boat either from Indonesia or New Guinea. Well before Cook was sent in the *Endeavour* to explore the possible "great south land", other explorers had struck the coastline. Dutch merchants, who often arrived by accident while sailing to the Dutch East Indies (now Indonesia), first began to arrive from 1606, including Willem Jansz, Dirk Hartog, Willem de Vlamingh, Jan Carstenz and many more. Portuguese navigators, such as de Quiros and de Torres, added to the knowledge of "New Holland's" coastline. Cook, however, did claim Australia's east coast as British territory on 22 August 1770 at Possession Island, Queensland — paving the way for colonisation. French navigators Louis de Bougainville, Nicolas Baudin and La Pérouse also visited before colonisers on the First Fleet arrived to settle the continent in 1788.

STATES & TERRITORIES

Following European settlement, Australia became a British penal colony and was split up into a number of States. Each State had different laws, policies and military forces. In 1901, the six States in existence decided to unite in Federation, which gave them an over-arching legal, political, governmental and defence system. Today, Australia has six States — New South Wales, Western Australia, Queensland, Victoria, Tasmania and South Australia — and two Territories, the Northern Territory and the Australian Capital Territory, as well as sea territory.

the FACTS!

"ADVANCE AUSTRALIA FAIR", Australia's national anthem, was written by Scotsman Peter Dodds McCormick under the pen name of Amicus and was first performed on 30 November 1878. It became the official national anthem in 1984. The original lyrics were "Australian sons let us rejoice".

AUSTRALIA'S SEA TERRITORY (the Economic Exclusion Zone) is 8,148,250 km^2 — more than the country's land mass.

ONLY TWO ACTIVE VOLCANOES are within Australian territory. The largest is Big Ben on Heard Island, which is closer to Antarctica than to Australia. It was last active in 1987. The other is on McDonald Island and last erupted in 2005. On the mainland, the last volcanic activity occurred a few thousand years ago at Mount Gambier, South Australia.

THE LONGEST RIVER is the Murray River, which flows through New South Wales and South Australia and is 2520 km long. The longest continuous system is the Murray–Darling, at 3370 km long.

AN ABUNDANCE of highly combustible eucalypts makes Australia one of the most fire prone places on Earth. Bushfires costs Australia millions of dollars each year.

Below: Australia's long, largely sand-fringed coastline makes relaxing on the beach a national pastime.

5

A continental,
prehistoric ark

the FACTS!

SOME PEOPLE THINK pterosaurs and pterodactyls (above) were birds, but they are neither birds nor dinosaurs, but winged reptiles that lived during the Age of Dinosaurs.

AUSTRALIA IS STILL DRIFTING north at about the same rate as human fingernails grow.

AROUND 140 MILLION YEARS ago, during the early Cretaceous Period, Australia was already so flat that a shallow inland sea spread over the land. Marine dinosaurs, such as dolphin-like ichthyosaurs and huge mosasaurs, swam in the sea along with giant salamander-like amphibians, enormous sharks, crocodile-like reptiles and turtles.

IN 1903, Australia's first dinosaur fossil, which was a claw from a carnivorous theropod dinosaur, was discovered by a geologist at Cape Patterson, Victoria.

LARK QUARRY, Queensland, preserves the world's best evidence of a dinosaur stampede. Hundreds of footprints of running coelurosaur dinosaurs are fossilised in the mud.

ONLY A SINGLE ARM bone of a ceratopsian dinosaur (similar to Triceratops) has been found here. Amusingly, the 2-m-long *Serendipaceratops arthurclarkei* is named after science fiction author Arthur C Clarke.

Below: The fossilised bones of marine dinosaurs have been found in places where the Cretaceous inland sea once covered western Queensland.

Australia was not always a drifting island continent, for aeons it was part of the supercontinent known as Gondwanaland, which also included Africa, South America, India and Antarctica. Around 60 million years ago, Australia broke free from Antarctica and began gradually drifting north.

THIS CONTINENTAL ARK carried with it prehistoric plants and animals that, due to the isolation, sometimes evolved very differently from those in other places in the world. In some cases, isolation even led to the unique fauna and flora that we see today. The continent also carried with it fossil evidence from as far back as the Triassic Period (250–205 million years ago), which helps palaeontologists obtain a picture of dinosaurs that roamed Gondwanaland at the time. The first fossil was found in 1903, but many more fossils have since been discovered across Australia. Creatures from the huge sauropods (herbivorous dinosaurs) to the fierce, carnivorous *Ozraptor subotaii* (known from just a single bone found near Geraldton in Western Australia), have been revealed.

Above: Wollemi National Park, NSW, is where the ancient Wollemi Pine was discovered in 1994. The plant belongs to the 200-million-year-old Araucariaceae family.

RULING REPTILES

Dinosaurs belong to a group of reptiles that are known as archosaurs, which means "ruling reptiles". They were highly successful beasts that roamed the Earth and swam in the seas for more than 180 million years until a mass extinction, known as the Cretaceous–Tertiary

Boundary, occurred around 65 million years ago. No one is yet sure exactly why the dinosaurs died out, but numerous theories have been put forward, including volcanoes altering the climate, a meteorite impact causing a "nuclear winter" (an intensely cold snap in which tsunamis ravaged the shores and fires burnt across the land) or a combination of such events.

ANCIENT LIFE FORMS

The world's oldest known fossils are single-celled cyanobacteria known as stromatolites, which are found in Hamelin Pool at Shark Bay, Western Australia. Stromatolites have existed for around 3.5 billion years, although the ones in Hamelin Pool are relatively young and date to only around 3000 years old. They grow extremely slowly, with some growing less than 0.4 mm a year.

Right: Stromatolites may look like rocks, but they are actually single-celled cyanobacteria that are known as "living fossils".

Above: Diprotodon grew to about 1.7 m tall and could have weighed as much as 2.5 tonnes. Although it resembled a very large wombat, it has no close relatives living today.

Top, right: Thylacoleo carnifex was the largest carnivore ever to have lived in Australia. Amazingly, this marsupial lion is more closely related to the Koala and wombats than to other marsupials.

FROM BIG THINGS, LITTLE THINGS GROW

After the demise of the dinosaurs, other gigantic prehistoric animals, known as "megafauna", lived in Australia — some were the distant ancestors of today's much smaller Australian fauna, such as kangaroos and the Emu. Megafauna were not dinosaurs, but simply huge mammals (some were even marsupials), birds or reptiles that walked the Earth up until 40,000–30,000 years ago, meaning that when Aborigines first arrived in Australia, some megafauna still existed. Some scientists believe that climate change coupled with human hunting could have been responsible for the demise of these creatures. Stone tools found with the remains of the goanna-like "Great Ripper" Lizard *Megalania* add weight to the theory that Aborigines may have hunted the large, slow-moving megafauna. Today, the Red Kangaroo (*Macropus rufus*) is Australia's largest kangaroo, but once the 3-m-tall *Procoptodon goliah* was king of the kangaroos. It could weigh several hundred kilograms and, rather than browsing as modern kangaroos do, probably used its long arms to pull branches from the trees and feed on fruit and leaves. Huge, flightless "thunder birds" also lived in parts of the world. Similar to the modern Emu, the formidable *Genyornis newtoni,* Australia's megafauna bird, inhabited arid woodlands and grasslands.

Right: Palaeontologists from Queensland Museum carefully extricate fossils from the rocks so they can be studied and preserved.

the FACTS!

BECAUSE DINOSAURS were so big, many scientists first believed that they must have had two brains — one in the head to control the front of the body and another in the pelvis to control the back. However, this was not the case and we now know that even dinosaurs only had one brain.

IN 1999, THE SKELETON of an elasmosaur, a marine dinosaur, was found by two fisherman in Tropical North Queensland. The fossil, which has been nicknamed "Dave", was incredibly well preserved and up to 80% of its skeleton was recovered. Unfortunately, Dave's head was not found and is still missing.

ONE OF THE CONTINENT'S strangest-looking dinosaurs was the heavily armour-plated *Minmi paravertebra*, which lived from 110–100 million years ago. *Minmi* was covered in bony plates known as oesteoderms (similar to the skin of today's crocodiles). A skeleton of this primitive ankylosaur is the most complete fossil skeleton ever found in Australia.

LUNGFISH, such as the endangered Queensland Lungfish (*Neoceratodus forsteri*), belong to a 390-million-year-old early Devonian group of fish known as the Sarcopterygii; for this reason, they are sometimes known as "living fossils".

HADROSAURS, or duck-billed dinosaurs, may have made loud honks or hooting sounds by passing air through the unusual chamber and bellow-like structures in their skulls. Noise would be created in a similar fashion to people blowing into a wind instrument. Australia's most famous duck-billed dinosaur is *Muttaburrasaurus langdoni*, which was discovered by pastoralist Doug Langdon in Queensland's Channel Country in 1963.

Ancient
Indigenous heritage

Above: Aboriginal artist Emma Nungurayi.

Above, top to bottom: Boomerangs were used for hunting and as a tool; Nulla nullas had the same use; Rhythm clapsticks for corroborees.

When Cook claimed Australia as British territory, the land was not uninhabited or "terra nullius" (no one's land) as claimed. Aborigines and Torres Strait Islander people have enjoyed a rich spiritual connection with the land for more than 60,000 years.

THE EARLIEST archaeological evidence of Aboriginal occupation is the body of a man nicknamed Mungo Man, which dates to 40,000 years ago; however, complex spiritual beliefs mean that most Aborigines see their occupation of Australia as timeless. When Europeans first arrived in Australia, an estimated 300,000–750,000 Aborigines probably inhabited the continent, living in groups of 50–2000 members who spoke the same language or similar dialects. Historians believe there may have been as many as 900 different "tribes" and more than 200 languages (each of which may have included several dialects) were spoken.

Aboriginal culture is the oldest continuous culture on Earth and, like many ancient cultures, it is oral not written. The best tools historians have to help reveal Australia's Indigenous heritage are the accounts of Aborigines and Torres Strait Islanders (passed on from generation to generation); Dreaming stories and legends; dances, songs and rituals; archaeological artefacts; rock art; and continuing customs and beliefs.

Below: Aboriginal men and children celebrate their culture in a parade in Brisbane, Qld.

TOOLS & TUCKER

Unlike the early European settlers, who struggled to survive in the harsh climate, Aborigines had long learned how to hunt and gather edible plants and animals. Indigenous peoples were not strictly nomadic but moved seasonally through their traditional territory, seeking permission from other tribes if they had to cross into another groups' lands. They were, and remain, excellent trackers who are able to identify animals by their prints and scats, and hunted them using boomerangs, spears, stone axes and woomeras (throwing clubs). For defence, Aborigines carried shields of timber and bark, carved or painted with symbolic designs. Women carried "dillybags" woven out of animal hair or grass, and one of the most important Aboriginal tools — the simple digging stick. This sharpened piece of hardwood was used to dig up termite mounds, roots, tubers, plants or burrowing animals, and even to spear fish and knock fruit from trees. Women also carried an oval-shaped vessel made of carved wood, known as a *coolamon*. It could be used for digging, containing food or even carrying a baby.

the FACTS!

ABORIGINES MADE stone tools with ground edges up to 10,000 years before European peoples did.

SOME INDIGENOUS PEOPLES, particularly those on Qld's Cape York, prohibit speaking during times of mourning and use a form of elaborate sign language instead.

ALTHOUGH IN ENGLISH we often use the word "tribe" to describe Aboriginal groups, today most Aborigines refer to those who speak the same language or live in the same area as "mobs". They may ask, "What mob do you belong to?" rather than, "Where do you come from?", as white Australians might.

TORRES STRAIT ISLANDERS and Aboriginal people are ethnically different. Torres Strait Islanders live on islands off the far north coast of Queensland, between Australia and New Guinea. Culturally, many Torres Strait Islander people share closer similarities to Papua New Guineans and other Pacific Islanders than to the many diverse Aboriginal groups throughout the mainland and Tasmania.

THE DREAMING

Central Australian Aborigines call the Dreaming *Alcheringa* and believe it has existed and continues to exist forever. It comprises the past, present and future and describes the intricate spiritual relationship between the landscape and landforms, the ancestors and spirits, the animals and plants, and the Aboriginal or Torres Strait Islander peoples. Most Aboriginal people believe that each individual is the descendant of a plant or animal, which is their totem, and that landscapes were created and formed out of the experiences of ancestor spirits. Thus, the spires of the Three Sisters were once women who were turned to stone to punish their father, and the movement of the huge Rainbow Serpent over the land was able to carve landscapes. The Dreaming stories also explain the complex web of kinship links and how an individual should interact with others according to tribal law and cultural taboos and customs. These spiritual beliefs are recorded and retold in rock art (above), which may serve to simultaneously record Aboriginal history, to decorate, and to inform those who visit the rock art galleries of particular stories and beliefs.

the FACTS!

HAROLD THOMAS, a Luritja man, designed the Aboriginal flag in 1971. The black section is symbolic of the Aboriginal people, while the red represents the Earth and the Aborigines' spiritual connection with it. The yellow circle is the sun, regarded as the giver of life.

ABORIGINES CREATED FIRE by rubbing sticks together to generate heat. It became extremely important to carry fire from one site to the next, usually with a smouldering "fire stick".

WHEN ABORIGINES remained in one spot semi-permanently or for the season, they usually constructed a bark hut (below) known as a *gunyah*, *wurley* or *humpy*.

SONG & DANCE

In Aboriginal culture, song and dance are crucial elements to relay stories, legends and belief systems. Ritualistic or celebratory corroborees (an Aboriginal word for ceremonies) are also imperative for maintaining the Indigenous way of life. Most songs are very short, but may be linked with other songs to tell the Dreamings. Songs are considered very powerful and may be restricted to certain occasions or only sung (or heard) by certain people. Restrictions also apply to some dances. Songs and dances are often accompanied by rhythmic clapsticks and the haunting melody of the didgeridoo. The didgeridoo was first created to attract Emus and is a 160-cm-long, 30-mm-wide piece of wood that has been hollowed out by termites. When correctly blown into, it creates a droning, trumpet-like tune. Playing the "didj" correctly requires mastering continuous breathing, in which air is drawn in through the nose so the player does not have to stop to take a breath. Bullroarers were also used in some ceremonies and were believed to make the noise of the spirits by some groups; others considered them simply toys. Bullroarers are composed of a flat piece of wood attached to string, and, when swung around, make a loud, whirring noise.

BUNGAREE, a Ku-ring-gai man from north Sydney Harbour, became the first Aborigine to circumnavigate Australia when he sailed with Matthew Flinders in 1801–1802.

ABORIGINES WERE NOT included in the Commonwealth census until after 27 May 1967. The Australian Constitution had stated, "In reckoning the number of people in the Commonwealth ... aboriginal natives shall not be counted".

THE EFFECTS of European settlement on Aborigines were devastating. Clashes between Aborigines and settlers led to bloodshed on both sides, although many more Aborigines than Europeans were killed. Contagious diseases also claimed the lives of many thousands of Indigenous people, who had no immunity to them. Aborigines were also displaced, separated from their kin and denied the rights of white Australians. Today, Australians are working towards reconciliation and improving living conditions in Aboriginal communities.

Who are the Aussies?

Above: This woman, with her Blue Heeler dog and Akubra® hat, may epitomise the stereotypical Aussie, but multiculturalism means that today's Aussie is often anything but typical.

Aside from the first Australians — the Indigenous peoples — many of the early Australians were sent to the nation against their will, as convicts. However, soon people began to see that they may be able to make a better life across the waves than they could in poverty-stricken Britain, and immigrants began to flock to Australia.

the FACTS!

ONLY ONE MEMBER of the First Fleet had visited Australia before. Fourteen-year-old Peter Hibbs had sailed into Botany Bay on the *Endeavour* and then returned aged 32 in 1788 as a seaman aboard the *Sirius.* He eventually made a life for himself in Australia, dying at Portland Head, NSW, in 1847.

PHILLIP SCHAEFFER arrived in Australia on the *Lady Juliana* in June 1790. He had been appointed superintendent of convicts, but on arriving in Sydney, Governor Phillip learned he spoke only German. He was given 56 acres on the banks of the Parramatta River and became Australia's first wine-maker.

IN 1828, there were 3.34 men to every woman in the colony.

CHINESE IMMIGRANTS comprised 3.3% of Australia's population in 1861. Amazingly, there were 38,337 Chinese men in Australia in 1861, but just eleven Chinese women.

AUSTRALIA'S INDIGENOUS population stands at around 483,000 at the time of publication.

WHEN WHITE PEOPLE first started to arrive, some of the Aborigines believed them to be the ghosts of ancestor spirits and many were friendly. However, once they realised that the white people were invading their lands, many, understandably, turned hostile. Following Cook's voyage on the *Endeavour,* it took eighteen years before Britain sent people to colonise the new land. The end of the American War of Independence in 1783 meant that Britain could no longer send their criminal undesirables to the Americas, and British gaols were overflowing. In May 1787, at the suggestion of esteemed botanist Joseph Banks (who had travelled on the *Endeavour* voyage with Cook), a fleet of eleven ships departed England, with more than 1400 souls on board, for the new penal settlement of Botany Bay. The site Banks had suggested was deemed unsuitable when the ships began to arrive in mid December 1787 and Captain Arthur Phillip, who had been assigned to govern the convicts and officers, moved the settlement to Port Jackson (Sydney Harbour) on 26 January 1788.

CROOKS & UNFORTUNATES

All up, between the first batch of convicts who arrived on the First Fleet in 1788 and the last, who disembarked from the *Hougoumont* in Fremantle on 10 January 1868, approximately 159,100 convicts were sent to Australia. Punishment in Britain at the time was harsh and few of the convicts were hardened criminals; most were petty thieves, frauds and prostitutes, but some were just destitute children. In the early years of settlement, the nation was ashamed of its criminal past and "emancipists" (freed convicts) and "exclusives" (free settlers) argued about who should be allowed to own land and vote. Many convicts were soon pardoned and worked hard to better themselves — some even became very wealthy. Today, most Aussies are proud to find they had a convict ancestor.

Below: Aborigines, bushies and sporty beach-goers all make up the face of the nation.

Above: In spite of divisive past immigration policies, today's Australia is a vibrant, multicultural nation that welcomes people of all races, religions and political beliefs — but asks that migrants similarly respect the country's democratic principles and Anglo-celtic influence.

A BETTER LIFE

Most of Australia's convicts were from the British Isles, Scotland and Ireland, others were prisoners from British India and the Caribbean. Australia's first free settlers arrived on the *Bellona* in January 1793, but it took years before many other settlers followed. Only around 14,000 free settlers had arrived by 1830, compared to more than 63,000 convicts. However, in 1832, facing high unemployment in Britain and a shortage of labour in Australia, the British government decided to provide funds for working-class emigrants to come to Australia, using money gathered from land sales in the new colony. Between 1830 and 1850, more than 173,000 free settlers arrived — compared to convict shipments of just 83,000. Most settlers were from the United Kingdom and southern Ireland and almost 75% of Australians can claim descent to British or Irish people.

IN THE EARLY YEARS of the 20th century, efforts were made to establish a Jewish homeland in Australia. The attempts failed, but many Jews also settled here and were integrated into Australian society. Numerous gold rushes further increased Australia's population and drew fortune-hunters from around the globe, including many Chinese and Japanese prospectors, and Indians, who made a living selling goods on the goldfields. Between 1864 and 1904, more than 57,000 Pacific Islanders, known as "Kanakas", were brought to Australia to

Right, top to bottom: Filipino people showcase their heritage at a multicultural parade that is part of Darwin Festival, NT; A man hands out Australian flags to eager patriots at an Australia Day parade in Brisbane, Qld.

work as labourers. Most came from the Solomon Islands and the New Hebrides and arrived in Australia to find they were little more than slaves.

While assisted immigration schemes were in place to attract white settlers, people were prejudiced against Asians and black people and laws were passed to restrict their immigration, which became known as the "White Australia Policy". Assisted immigration for whites continued for around 150 years and was only abolished in 1981. During the 1840s, it cost just £1 for adults on assisted passage to come to Australia and 10 shillings for children. Even from the 1940s to the 1980s it cost just £10 for adults and numerous "10-pound Poms" arrived. Greeks, Italians and other Europeans were also encouraged to emigrate. Australians now embrace all cultures and our immigration policy no longer discriminates by race, religion or country of origin.

the FACTS!

THE FIRST government-assisted immigrants were 50 girls who arrived on 31 July 1831 aboard the *Palamban*. The girls were from the Foundling Hospital at Cork, Ireland, and the aim was to balance up the disproportionate number of men and women in the colony and provide educated women to marry the ex-soldiers and officials.

AROUND 27% of Australians today were born overseas.

WHEN THE PREJUDICIAL *Immigration Restriction Act* was passed in 1901, immigration for Indians, black people and Asians all but ceased.

GERMAN, PRUSSIAN and Silesian emigrants, fleeing religious persecution, settled in Australia from the 1830s.

SINCE THE END of World War II, more than 675,000 refugees fleeing conflict in many different countries have been resettled in Australia.

IN 1925, THE BIG BROTHER MOVEMENT was formed as a way to bring teenage British emigrants to Australia. The movement sponsored the immigration of more than 1900 British youths between 1925 and 1929 and matched each one with an older Australian mentor.

MORE THAN 15% of Australians speak a language other than English at home.

Amazing
adventurers

Above: Hovell and Hume were astonished to see the snow-capped peaks of the Snowy Mountains.

the FACTS!

IN 1606, Portuguese navigator Luis Vaez de Torres discovered the passage now called the Torres Strait, but his discovery was kept secret for approximately 150 years.

DAMPIER WAS NOT a pirate by choice, but because his crew were running wild! Eventually, he escaped on the Nicobar Islands and miraculously sailed a canoe through rough storms to Sumatra.

WHEN BASS AND FLINDERS' tiny vessel capsized near Port Kembla, the two men defused a potentially hostile situation with Aborigines by showing them how to shave.

Above: Abel Tasman, the first European to discover Tasmania and New Zealand, later became a buccaneer and robbed Spanish vessels.

Below: Charles Sturt made a number of stoic missions into the vast deserts of Australia searching for an inland sea. It got so hot that the ink in the explorer's pens dried up!

Many daring navigators and overland adventurers explored the country's coasts and climes. Some were incredibly foolhardy and many lost their lives on their daring exploits, but all of them helped to define Australia's shape, extent and natural wonders.

THE FIRST EUROPEAN known to have seen Australian shores is Willem Jansz, who sailed the *Duyfken* into the Gulf of Carpentaria in 1606. However, it is possible that Chinese and Portuguese explorers knew of Australia's existence before then. Macassan traders from the Celebes, now known as Sulawesi, were also regular visitors to these shores to collect sea cucumbers and were known to the Aboriginal people.

Above: Privateer turned pirate William Dampier and the crew of the *Cygnet* spent two months on the Western Australian coast in 1688.

A STRANGE PAIR

Short, thin Matthew Flinders (right) and his portly, almost 2-m-tall friend George Bass were unlikely friends, but between them they chartered huge areas of Australia's coastline — even doing some of their sailing in a tiny 2.5 m sailing boat. In 1798, Bass sailed into the waters now known as Bass Strait, proving that Van Diemen's Land was indeed separate to the Australian mainland. His friend Flinders went on to be the first person to circumnavigate Van Diemen's Land and the Australian continent in 1802–1803. His well-travelled feline, Trim, accompanied him on his journeys and Flinders later wrote a biography of his cat's life and travels!

Right: Bass and Flinders braved the elements in the tiny *Tom Thumb II*.

Below: Many men sought to cross the formidable barrier of the Blue Mountains from as early as 1790, but the three men who went down in history as having successfully done so were William Wentworth (below left), Gregory Blaxland (below centre) and William Lawson (below right). The men stuck to the ridge tops, rather than stumble through the densely forested valleys, and reached the top of Mount York on 28 May 1813. Their expedition paved the way for extended grazing around the colony of New South Wales into the luxuriant grasslands of the Bathurst Plains.

Above, left to right: Edward Eyre and his loyal Aboriginal guide Wylie struggled across the Nullarbor Plain to Albany, WA, in 1841; Edmund Kennedy was searching for a suitable port on Cape York when he and his faithful Aboriginal friend Jackey Jackey were attacked by Aborigines. Despite Jackey Jackey trying to save his friend, Kennedy died; Robert O'Hara Burke and William Wills died on their mismanaged mission from Melbourne to Cooper Creek, Qld, in 1860–1861. Only one member of their party, John King, survived by living with Aborigines and was eventually rescued.

PHILLIP PARKER KING

The son of Governor Phillip Gidley King was a protege of Flinders and an eager adventurer. He sailed the *Mermaid* and the *Bathurst* around much of Australia's north and western coasts from 1817–1821, mapping over 2300 km of coastline.

SIR THOMAS MITCHELL

Stern Thomas Mitchell also believed, incorrectly, that Australia's interior hid an inland sea. He explored the Darling River and found "Australia Felix" in the good grazing lands of the Wimmera, and arable land in central Queensland.

JOHN OXLEY

Surveyor-General John Oxley discovered the "stupendous" Warrumbungle Range and the pastoral lands of New England in 1818. Later in his career he found the site for Brisbane and charted Queensland's Moreton Bay.

ALLAN CUNNINGHAM

Cunninghams Gap, which revealed the rich grasslands of the Darling Downs to this shy, sick botanist in 1827, was Cunningham's most major discovery. He is known for his determination as he almost failed many times but persevered.

LUDWIG LEICHHARDT

Eccentric Leichhardt traversed much of the tropical wilderness of Qld's Cape York, often living on bats, rats and anything else that would fit in his cooking pot. He eventually vanished in 1848 and the remains of his expedition party have never been found, despite extensive searches.

ERNEST GILES

Accomplished bushman Ernest Giles once devoured a dying baby wallaby "fur, skin, bones, skull and all" in his efforts to stay alive. He undertook many missions through formidable arid terrain in Central Australia from 1873–1876, finding the Gibson Desert and Lake Amadeus.

JOHN McKINLAY

When trapped by the floodwaters of the East Alligator River on his 1865 mission to the north, resourceful McKinlay built a rough raft by stretching the hides of his horses over a timber frame. Incredibly, the raft stayed afloat for six days, carrying the sixteen men to safety.

SIR DOUGLAS MAWSON

On 2 December 1911, Adelaide's Douglas Mawson led Australia's first polar expedition, which chartered 1500 km of coastline and up to 500 km of Macquarie Island. The men were the first to use morse code to communicate with the outside world from Antarctica.

Australia
rocks!

the FACTS!

ULURU (above) and Kata Tjuta (below) are all that remains of large blocks of stone known as inselbergs that existed in Central Australia about 600 million years ago and have since eroded.

THE STRIATED BEEHIVE DOMES of the Bungle Bungles, Western Australia, only came to the world's attention in 1982.

THE TREELESS NULLARBOR was once a sea floor that uplifted in the Miocene age, 25 million years ago.

THERE ACTUALLY IS no Great Dividing Range. Most of the Great Divide (which separates rivers that flow to Central Australia from those that flow to the Pacific) is flat land dotted with lakes. Only Victoria's Dargo High Plains, south of the Divide, comprise truly hilly country.

AT WOLFE CREEK, Western Australia, the world's second-largest known meteorite impact, which occurred about 300,000 years ago, has left a crater that is about 900 m in diameter and more than 46 m deep.

SOUTH AUSTRALIA'S Remarkable Rocks on Kangaroo Island (below) are the result of weathered granite.

Aeons of weathering and erosion of Australia's ancient land surface have carved incredible natural sculptures in rocks around Australia, creating geological phenomena that attract tourists from around the globe. Many are also places of great Aboriginal significance.

MOST GEOLOGISTS divide the continent into three distinct parts — the Eastern Highlands, the Central Lowlands and the Western Plateau. Beneath the Central Lowlands, the sedimentary rocks of the Great Artesian Basin trap water for this dry continent. The oldest rocks are found in the Western Plateau region (such as the Kimberley, Arnhem Land and Hamersley plateaus) with some being more than 3000 million years old. Of all the geological wonders found in Australia, the most bizarre are usually in sedimentary rock. The fantastic sandstone shapes of Blue Mountains National Park were once beds of mud beneath the basin of the sea, and the majestic rock of Uluru is actually layer upon layer of sedimentary sand that once washed down a raging river system. Chemical and weathering erosion ensure that, over centuries, part of all rock will become sediment that is transported by wind, waves or rivers to be deposited elsewhere. Other formations, such as the limestone Jenolan Caves, New South Wales, are formed of sediment that was once living coral reef.

Above: Wave Rock, WA, is made up of plutonic rock and was formed when the surrounding soil was some 11 m higher. The damp soil rotted away the granitic rock to form this shape.

Above: Over aeons, the sea has eroded the rock to sculpt the wave-cut sea stacks of the Twelve Apostles in Port Campbell National Park, Vic.

Below: The dramatic spires of The Pinnacles, WA, formed out of cemented grit of shell and coral debris and were left exposed when sand covering them was swept away.

Above: Wilpena Pound, SA, is a massive crater formed by the synclinal folding of quartzite rock, which has uplifted sections over millions of years.

Below: Undara volcanic lava tubes in Qld formed 190,000 years ago from the movement of honey-like lava through the earth. They are the world's longest from a single volcano.

The Great
Barrier Reef

The Great Barrier Reef, Queensland, is the only natural phenomonon that can be seen from space. It comprises some 3000 reefs composed of archipelagos of mainland islands, coral cays, fringing reefs and barrier reefs that drop off into the unfathomable depths of the continental shelf. The reef is home to an unparalleled abundance of marine life.

the FACTS!

THE GREAT BARRIER REEF covers an area of more than 300,000 km^2 — greater than that of the entire United Kingdom. It is the largest protected marine area in the world.

TODAY'S REEF is formed on the foundations of an older reef, which began growing more than 10,000 years ago.

Above: Scuba divers marvel at the many corals, which are not rocks but living organisms.

Above: A Common Lionfish is extremely well camouflaged amid the sea fans and soft coral.

INCREDIBLE ENGINEERING

Because of its global importance for species diversity, the reef was one of Australia's first World Heritage Areas, being inscribed in 1981. It also holds the distinction of being the largest structure ever built entirely by living creatures. It has been constructed, over a time scale of millions of years, from the limestone deposits of billions of tiny coral polyps working in symbiosis with bacteria that were able to convert sunlight to energy via photosynthesis. Together, this remarkable team of engineers created the elaborate reef we admire today. More than 600 spectacularly varied types of coral adorn the reef and attract around 1600 species of fish, 3000 molluscs and innumerable invertebrates.

THE CROWN-OF-THORNS Sea Star caused severe damage to about 17% of the Great Barrier Reef from the 1970s to 1990. Two major coral-bleaching events have also occurred, in 1998 and 2002.

SCIENTISTS AT JAMES COOK University in Townsville, Qld, are studying how the rare Longfin Batfish (*Platax pinnatus*) may help the Great Barrier Reef recover from overfishing. In laboratory tests simulating the effects of overfishing, choking seaweed quickly spread over the coral. The only fish shown to make a significant dent in the algal growth, allowing the coral to grow again, were Longfin Batfish, which usually eat invertebrates and plankton. Unfortunately, these fish are vulnerable to attack by spear fishers and habitat destruction of mangroves, where they breed.

Clockwise from above: Small fish swim above branching soft corals and brain corals; The vibrant Harlequin Tuskfish; Emperor Angelfish; A colourful sea hare.

Australia's
amazing World Heritage

Some of the continent's unique or pristine habitats are so special — either as links to our evolutional or cultural past or as hotspots of biodiversity or geological activity — that they are preserved as World Heritage Areas.

Above: **Beautiful Kakadu teems with life after seasonal rains.**

the FACTS!

IN 2000, the imposing terrain of the Greater Blue Mountains was inscribed on the World Heritage List. They comprise 1.03 million ha in eight protected areas, including seven national parks. The area protects 13% of the world's eucalypt species (the oil of which diffuses into the air, creating the blue haze) and dramatic rock formations, such as the Three Sisters (above).

THE WET TROPICS, Qld, comprise an 894,000 ha area that is one of the most spectacular regions of rainforest diversity known to man. They were inscribed in 1988 as an example of "superlative natural phenomena" and to conserve biological diversity, among other things. At least 390 plant species and 25 animal species found in the Wet Tropics are considered rare.

SEVENTEEN PLACES have been honoured by a World Heritage listing, with two of them being man-made (Sydney Opera House and the Royal Exhibition Building) and another comprising two important fossil sites (Australian Mammal Fossil Sites). The most famous are probably the Great Barrier Reef, and Kakadu (right) — spectacular RAMSAR-listed wetlands of floral and faunal abundance, where one-quarter of Australia's bird species are found. Also found there are 132 reptile species, more than 60 mammals, 25 frogs, 55 freshwater fish and more than 10,000 insects! During the wet season, torrents cascade off the 500-m-long Arnhem Land Plateau to fill the wetlands and water the ravines, which are verdant with *Allosyncarpia* trees found nowhere else on the planet. More than 30 floral species in the Stone Country are also considered rare or endemic. So rich is Kakadu's bounty that the area has sustained Indigenous Australians for at least 25,000 years, possibly many more.

ROCK OF AGES

Rivalling Kakadu in fame is the enormous crimson monolith of Uluṟu (bottom left) and the 36 weathered domes of Kata Tjuṯa, which were inscribed in two stages for their natural and cultural values. Culturally, they are an important site for the Pitjantjatjara people, also known as the Anangu, who have woven elaborate Dreaming stories around these spiritually captivating structures. Geologically, the awe-inspiring sandstone rocks have risen from the surrounding plain as erosion wore down the surrounding softer rock.

BIODIVERSITY HOTSPOT

Three intersecting climactic zones resulted in the incredible biodiversity of the stunning Shark Bay World Heritage Area (below) — 2.3 million ha on the western-most point of the Australian coast. Flora is particularly abundant in the region, which supports around 283 species of vascular plants. Off the coast, extensive seagrass beds provide nourishment for the endangered Dugong and around 10,000 of them visit these waters, along with Humpback Whales, marine turtles and countless marine invertebrates.

WILD TASMANIA

One of Australia's largest World Heritage Areas is the 1.38 million ha Tasmanian Wilderness, which was inscribed in 1982 and covers 20% of the island. So rich is the plant life of this largely pristine wilderness that the IUCN recognises it as an International Centre for Plant Diversity and the area protects a high number of endemic species that are relics from Gondwanan times. Some of the Tasmanian wilderness areas also constitute important cultural sites that preserve Aboriginal rock art dating back to the last Ice Age, around 18,000 years ago.

Above, left to right: Cradle Mountain and Dove Lake in the Tasmanian Wilderness WHA; Lord Howe Island, off the NSW coast; Heritage-listed Fraser Island contains the only tall rainforest growing on sand dunes anywhere in the world.

the FACTS!

WORLD-HERITAGE-LISTED Lord Howe Island, 700 km north-east of Sydney, NSW, was inscribed in 1982 and includes Admiralty Islands, Mutton Bird Islands, Balls Pyramid and Lord Howe. It formed when an underwater volcano arose about 7 million years ago and contains lush rainforest and palm forests surrounded by the most southerly coral reef system. Lord Howe Island protects an astonishing 105 endemic plant species.

IN JUNE 2003, the outstanding natural values of Purnululu National Park, WA, earned it a place on the World Heritage List. The park contains the striated beehive-like sedimentary rocks of the 45,000 ha Bungle Bungle Range. *Livistona* palms flourish in the ravines that provide protection for Rainbow Bee-eaters, Red-backed Fairy-wrens and Great Bowerbirds.

MACQUARIE ISLAND, within the Australian Exclusive Economic Zone, was inscribed in 1997 as an example of unique geodiversity and "superlative natural phenomena". It is the only island on the planet to be made up wholly of rocks from the mantle of the Earth and the oceanic crust — plate tectonics and continental drift having thrust them above the Earth's surface around 30–11 million years ago.

HEARD AND MCDONALD ISLANDS, 1500 km north of Antarctica, make up some of the wildest habitat ever discovered and received World Heritage status in 1997. They are made up of glacial ice covering the outcrops of live, still-smoking volcanoes.

LAKE'S LINK TO THE PAST

A system of Pleistocene era lakes that cover more than 240,000 ha make up the World-Heritage-listed Willandra Lakes in New South Wales. They provide "exceptional testimony to a past civilisation" because the 40,000-year-old bones of an Aborigine, nicknamed Mungo Man, were found here, as well as other examples of Aboriginal ceremonial cremation and burial. Willandra Lakes is also an important conservation site, with 22 recorded mammal species and 137 bird species.

RELICS FROM GONDWANA

Over 100 million years ago, flowering plants (angiosperms) developed and spread, and today, Australia's World-Heritage-listed Gondwana Rainforests preserve a direct link to that phase of floral evolution. First inscribed in 1986, the area was extended in 1994 to include 366,507 ha of the former Australian East Coast Subtropical and Temperate Rainforest Parks, along with scattered patches of rainforest in South-East Queensland. It protects the largest area of subtropical rainforest on Earth.

Above, left to right: The barren "lunettes" of Lake Mungo provide archaeological evidence of Australia's human and evolutional change; The mossy green rainforest of Lamington National Park, part of the Gondwana Rainforests that stretch from Newcastle, NSW, to near Brisbane, Qld.

ISLAND MADE OF SAND

The largest sand island in the world, Fraser Island, Queensland (left), was inscribed in 1992. Up to 70,000 years of climate and sea level fluctuations are recorded in the sediments of the island's massive dunes (some up to 240 m high), which continue to evolve and shift with the elements. Coupled with the dunes are barrow lakes, window lakes and 40 perched lakes, which make up half the world's total number of such depressions. Fraser Island is also home to Australia's only purebred Dingoes.

Marvellous
mammals

Above: DNA evidence shows the Dingo is related to the Indian wolf. It was introduced to Australia around 3000 years ago.

the FACTS!

ABORIGINES used the Dingo as a companion animal and it was known as *warrigal* in some languages. The expression "three-dog night" arose because Aborigines curled up with Dingoes to keep them warm on cold winter nights.

WOMBATS KILL PREDATORS that follow them down the burrow by using their bottoms to crush pursuers against the burrow's roof. Rather than being "muddle-headed", wombats have a much larger brain, proportionally, than any other marsupial and are quite intelligent.

IN 2004, researchers at the Australian National University found a chain of odd sex chromosomes that point to a possible link between the Platypus and birds.

DESPITE SIMILARITIES with birds, male Short-beaked Echidnas, ejaculate in a similar way to reptiles, using only half of the penis. Reptiles have a pair of penises, known as hemipenes, and copulate using only one at a time.

THE RED KANGAROO (*Macropus rufus*, below) is Australia's largest native mammal. Males can grow up to 1.5 m tall and weigh 85 kg.

Australia is the only place on Earth where all three groups of mammals — marsupial, placental and monotreme — coexist. Up to 95% of Australia's unique mammals are found nowhere else.

THE BEST KNOWN, and many say cutest, Australian mammal is the Koala (*Phascolarctos cinereus*). Koalas do not need to drink, except during drought. Usually they obtain all of the moisture they require from the toxic gum leaves they eat, which they break down using a specialised appendix-like structure known as a caecum. In the past, people believed that Koalas got drunk on gum leaves and that is why they slept so much. In fact, gum leaves provide little nutritional value, so the Koala must conserve energy by sleeping for up to 20 hours a day. Koalas' closest living relatives are wombats, which live on the ground where they use their sturdy claws to construct deep burrows. Like Koalas, wombats have backwards-facing pouches, but they eat roots and grass and their young walk once they leave the burrow and never ride on mum's back.

Above: The Koala is not a bear; it is a marsupial that gives birth to a tiny furless joey, which remains in a backwards-facing pouch until old enough to cling, piggyback-style, to its mother. *Below:* Koalas' closest relatives are wombats.

MISSING-LINK MAMMALS

Australia's two bizarre monotremes were considered miraculous additions to biology when they were first discovered, and some evolutionary biologists regard them as the primitive "missing link" between reptiles and mammals. The word monotreme translates as "one hole" as, like reptiles, they have only one opening (known as a cloaca) for their waste and reproductive purposes. Also like reptiles, they lay eggs and are the only known mammals to do so. However, as for all mammals, they are covered in fur (the echidna's spines being a type of modified hair) and they feed their young on milk that seeps from glands on the mother's belly. The Platypus (*Ornithorhynchus anatinus,* below) is a water-dwelling mammal, but is able to use its webbed feet to waddle awkwardly on land. It uses its highly sensitive bill to feel for the weak electrical impulses generated by the movement of its prey. The Short-beaked Echidna (*Tachyglossus aculeatus,* above) is a terrestrial creature that is able to curl itself up into a tight, spiny ball if threatened. It feeds exclusively on ants and termites.

FREQUENTLY SEEN MAMMALS

Many of Australia's mammals have, over time, become accustomed to sharing their habitats with humans and are often seen around backyards, campsites and nature reserves. Kangaroos and the smaller wallabies are frequent visitors to golf courses or parks and even the small, shy pademelons (above left) regularly appear at dusk around forest fringes and will grant an audience to quiet, respectful individuals. The more raucous Common Ringtail (*Pseudocheirus peregrinus*) and Common Brushtail (*Trichosurus vulpecula*, above centre) are even known to enter people's houses and build a drey in the ceiling. They are daring, noisy scavengers of orchard trees and rubbish bins. Australian Fur-seals (*Arctocephalus pusillus doriferus*) and Australian Sea-lions (*Neophoca cinerea*, above right) were once hunted for their pelts, but are now protected. Millions of visitors each year delight at their clumsy, gregarious antics when they visit rocky shorelines and breeding colonies off Australia's southern coast.

AIRBORNE MAMMALS

The only true flying mammals are bats (right), which have lightweight, modified skeletons and membranous skin stretched over their elongated fingers and forearms. Bats have existed in Australia for at least 50 million years and scientists believe they may have evolved from small, shrew-like South American mammals that were able to glide. However, Australia is also home to another group of mammalian aerialists — the gliders. While they cannot propel themselves through the air with true flight, a thin membrane of skin (known as a patagium), which stretches from their forelimbs to their ankles, enables them to "volplane" from tree to tree. Australia has three groups of gliding possums — greater gliders, tiny feathertail gliders (above left) and wrist-wringed gliders, such as the commonly seen Sugar Glider (*Petaurus breviceps*).

DOLPHINS & DAUGHTERS

In 2005, Dr Michael Krutzen at the University of New South Wales discovered that female bottlenose dolphins studied at Shark Bay, WA, seem to be passing on the knowledge of how to use a tool to their daughters. Some female dolphins learned to poke their beaks into a broken-off, cup-shaped piece of sponge and used it to lure fish out of hiding on the craggy sea floor. Not all dolphins did this, however, and researchers found that the females that did were related mothers and daughters, suggesting it was a learned trait. Only one male used the tool, and researchers think that may be because males are too busy seeking out partners to bother learning to "sponge".

the FACTS!

THE TASMANIAN DEVIL has exceptionally strong jaws and teeth that make it capable of eating an entire sheep, skull and all.

THE LARGE-FOOTED MYOTIS (*Myotis macropus*) is known as the "fishing bat" and is one of the smallest mammals in the world, at just 2.5 cm long. It has exceptionally large claws to seize and grasp its prey and fishes in the dark, using echolocation to detect the ripples of prey in the water.

THE MILK of the Tammar Wallaby (*Macropus eugenii*) could prove a breakthrough in medical research because it contains an anti-bacterial that has been found to be 100 times more powerful than penicillin. Scientists working at the Department of Primary Industry Research Centre at Atwood, Victoria, discovered the anti-bacterial component in 2007.

AN EASTERN PYGMY-POSSUM (*Cercartetus nanus*) being studied in Fritz Geiser's lab at the University of New England in Armidale, New South Wales, has broken the world record for the longest known mammal hibernation. It slept for a record 367 days! While asleep, it used just one-fortieth of the energy it required when awake.

MALE ANTECHINUSES and phascogales (below) — small carnivorous marsupials known as dasyurids — only survive for one mating season. They expend so much energy having sex that they have no energy left to live!

Incredible
insects & spiders

Above: The female Cairns Birdwing Butterfly (*Ornithoptera priamus*) is Australia's largest butterfly with a wingspan of up to 18 cm.

There are more insects in Australia than all the other types of animal combined. In fact, the typical suburban garden probably contains as many insects as there are humans living in your State.

the FACTS!

OUT OF ALL OF THE EARTH'S animals, 90% are insects.

A FLY'S FEET are covered in tiny tastebuds that are 10 million times more sensitive than a human's.

BEES AND WASPS have such an excellent sense of smell that scientists are training them to work in a similar way to sniffer dogs.

RHINOCEROS BEETLES are exceptionally strong — they can lift 850 times their own weight!

SOME PEOPLE incorrectly believe that butterflies live for just one day, but some survive for many months.

A GROUP OF MALE CICADAS can sing so loudly that they can reach more than 120 decibels, about the same noise as a loud rock band.

A FLEA'S JUMP is equivalent to a human jumping 250 m into the air.

THERE ARE MORE species of insects that eat green plants on the Earth than species of green plants!

MOST SPIDERS are cannibalistic; some even eat their own mothers!

THERE ARE AROUND 30,000 known species of spider, but scientists estimate a further 90,000 may yet be discovered.

ANTS ARE TINY, but there are so many of them that the weight of all the ants on Earth is greater than the weight of all of the humans on Earth.

"CUT UP" CREATURES

The name insect is derived from the Latin *insectum*, which means "cut up"; it describes the way the insect's body is divided into three distinct parts — the head, thorax and abdomen. Insects are invertebrates, which means they do not possess an internal skeleton or spinal chord but rather an "exoskeleton", which is usually a keratinous casing or shell that protects the body. Invertebrates are the most successful group of animals on Earth and include insects such as bugs, beetles and butterflies, as well as other animals such as spiders, leeches and worms. Insects existed 200 million years before the dinosaurs appeared and most are so superbly adapted that they will probably survive long after the human race has become extinct. Australia's isolation means that we have many unique insects and spiders. Some are extremely primitive and have survived here for the last 150 million years; others are new adaptations or arrivals. The earliest insects were "decomposers", which fed on decaying plant matter. They were followed by chewing insects and sapsuckers, which survived on the leaves and sap of plants. Once flowering plants (known as angiosperms) evolved millions of years later, pollinators and nectar-eaters, such as bees and butterflies, began to appear. Many insects have a few different life stages and may start out as caterpillar-like larvae, pupae or, in the case of dragonflies, free-swimming nymphs. Insects are crucial for life on Earth because they are a food source for many animals and numerous plant species rely on insects for pollination.

Above, top to bottom: Ferocious female mantids may eat the male before, during or after mating; Aborigines believe Leichhardt's Grasshopper is a creation spirit known as Lightning Man; For insects, European Honey Bees (*Apis mellifera*) have long memories. They can remember a flower's location even after two months of hibernation.

Fabulous frogs

*Frogs belong to the class Amphibia, which is the only class of animals able to live partly in water and partly on land. Approximately 220 native frog species are found in Australia, along with one introduced species, the poisonous Cane Toad (*Rhinella marina, *formerly* Bufo marinus*).*

FROGGY FAMILIES

Six frog families exist in Australia — Hylidae (tree-frogs), Myobatrachidae (water frogs), Limnodynastidae (ground frogs), Microhylidae (narrow-mouthed frogs), Ranidae ("true" frogs) and Bufonidae ("true" toads). Of these, the tree-frogs are the most conspicuous and abundant and Australia has most of the 830 known tree-frog species. Tropical rainforests are a haven for frog species, with approximately one-quarter of Australia's frog species found there.

Above: In dry times, Green Tree-frogs (*Litoria caerulea*) have been known to make toilet bowls their homes.

Left: The Water-holding Frog (*Cyclorana platycephala*) stores water in its bladder and aestivates for long periods below ground, appearing only after rain.

AMPHIBIAN "CANARIES"

Frogs are very susceptible to changes in climate and have long been regarded as the "canary in the gold mine" for environmental catastrophe. Usually, when frogs begin to decline, other organisms follow closely behind. Unfortunately, a disease caused by the chytrid fungus has been decimating frog populations since 1998, leaving some Australian ecosystems extremely vulnerable.

A STRANGE LIFE CYCLE

Frogs are egg-layers that undergo a number of changes in body form over their life cycle, depending on the species. Tadpoles typically undergo 46 different stages before they become frogs. Some frogs that live in dry or semi-arid areas have to take advantage of infrequent wet conditions and grow from tadpoles to frogs extremely quickly. In other species, the tadpoles may take more than a year to turn into frogs. Some inventive species have developed ways to avoid the need for water in egg-laying; instead spawning their eggs under leaf litter or carrying them in a pouch or in their stomachs.

A MOTHER OF A MOUTH

Australia was once home to the remarkable Southern Gastric-brooding Frog (*Rheobatrachus silus*, left), which was discovered in 1973 but has been extinct since the 1980s. Tadpoles developed inside the stomach of the mother for around six months and were then "born" through her mouth. In 2013, researchers from the University of NSW successfully cloned embryos of the species.

the FACTS!

LABYRINTHODONTS were early, salamander-like amphibians that lived more than 300 million years ago and grew to a maximum of 5 m.

ALL FROG SPECIES shed their skin about once or twice a week, and then eat it!

A FROG HAS ONLY nine vertebrae and the ones at the bottom of the backbone are fused to form a long bone known as the "urostyle".

MANY SCIENTISTS believe that frogs are likely to be the first animals to have developed vocal chords.

NOT ALL Australian tree-frogs live in trees; some are ground-dwellers and some even burrow.

SOME OF AUSTRALIA'S smallest native frogs are the tiny tree-frogs and toadlets ranging in size from 1.4–2 cm. The largest are the Giant Barred Frogs (*Mixophyes iteratus*), which grow to around 11.5 cm long.

BURROWING FROGS in the *Notaden* genus secrete a type of sticky glue to trap insects on their skin when they are above ground. Scientists at the University of Adelaide are investigating ways to use the "super-glue" substance as a natural medical adhesive to repair torn cartilage in human knee injuries.

THE POUCHED FROG (*Assa darlingtoni*) is sometimes also known as the Marsupial Frog because the male of the species carries its tadpoles with it in a special pouch. It is definitely not a marsupial, but scientists believe the tadpoles may absorb oxygen from the father's blood-vessel rich skin.

AUSTRALIA EVEN HAS A Cave-dwelling Frog (*Litoria cavernicola*) that lives among boulders and in caves in the Kimberley, WA.

Beautiful
birds

Above: Rainbow Lorikeets (*Trichoglossus haematodus*) are sociable birds that commonly fly in to parks and campsites seeking seeds or nectar.

the FACTS!

THREE SPECIES of mound-building birds live in Australia — the Australian Brush-turkey, Malleefowl and Orange-footed Scrubfowl. Males of all species pay careful attention to the nest, using their beaks as thermometers to ensure the nest stays at around 34 °C.

THE LAUGHING KOOKABURRA (*Dacelo novaeguineae*, top right) may seem like a happy, fun-loving bird, but hatchlings in the nest have specially hooked beaks designed for trying to kill their weaker siblings.

IN THE WILD the Budgerigar is found only in Australia and is always green and yellow. However, it is the world's most colourful bird because breeding in captivity has introduced thousands of budgie colour forms.

AUSTRALIA'S SMALLEST BIRD is the Mallee Emu-wren (*Stipiturus mallee*).

EMUS (*Dromaius novaehollandiae*) have a poorly developed claw on the end of each of their flightless wings. These claws appear to have no purpose.

AUSTRALIA'S Black Swan is the world's only black swan.

THE UNIQUE Magpie Goose has no close avian relatives. It has some duck-like and some goose-like features and its scientific name *Anseranas semipalmata* translates as "half-webbed goose-duck".

About 9800 bird species live on Earth and around 850 dwell in Australia, with 750 native to this continent or its island territories. Of these, the most famous are Australia's parrots and the continent was sometimes labelled as the "land of parrots" in old navigational maps because of the abundance of these brightly coloured birds.

BIRDS ARE DISTINGUISHED by one feature alone — their feathers, which set them apart from all other animals. Most birds are covered in many thousands of feathers. The tiny hummingbird has the fewest, at around 1000, while large swans have as many as 40,000. Birds also all lay eggs and have a modified, combined mouth and nose that we call a beak. Australian endemic birds range in size from the stately, flightless Emu to tiny emu-wrens and finches. They occupy habitats as diverse as the Antarctic islands (in the case of penguins), to semi-arid and savannah grasslands (Budgerigars) to dense rainforests (for fig-parrots and fruit-doves). Some, such as albatrosses and frigatebirds, spend most of their lives on the wing, soaring above the ocean, and come to shore only to lay eggs.

FLAMIN' GALAHS

Most Australians and travellers to this country have at some stage been amused by the seemingly inane antics of the Galah (*Cacatua roseicapilla*). These pink and grey characters are distributed across much of the continent, largely in semi-arid areas where little rain falls. When it does, they carry on like the proverbial "flamin' Galah" — swinging upside down from power lines, shaking the water from their feathers or rolling in the mud and dust. They are cheeky, lively birds and have even been seen letting themselves be sucked into spirals of small "willy willys" (wind tunnels), apparently just for fun.

BIRDS IN A BOWER

Bowerbirds are the avian architects of Australia. All eight species construct elaborate stage, avenue, maypole or mat bowers using vegetation, shells, flowers, moss or blue objects, depending on the species. Bowers are not nests — they are platforms either for dancing or displaying objects to attract females. The shiny male Satin Bowerbird (*Ptilonorhynchus violaceus*, above) collects blue objects; milk bottle tops are one of its favourite interior design materials.

LORDS OF THE DANCE

Lothario lyrebirds and graceful Brolgas are the nation's two most balletic birds. Lyrebirds (below right) scratch together a stage and then pull their shimmering veil of tail feathers over their heads and literally shimmy and "shake a tail feather" to impress females. Australia has two lyrebird species and both are also skilled mimics that can even recreate the sounds of chainsaws. The tall, elegant Brolga (*Grus rubicunda,* left) is a type of crane that greets other Brolgas with a stately bow, with its large grey wings outstretched, then prances up and down, flapping its wings.

Rapacious reptiles

Above: Pig-nosed Turtle.

Left: Marbled Velvet Gecko.

Reptiles were the first vertebrates to be able to emerge from the water and live on land, having evolved from amphibians in the Permian Period, some 300 million years ago. They are distinguished by being ectothermic (also known as cold-blooded) and by their covering of scales. Australia currently has around 840 known reptile species.

Above, left to right: One of Australia's most spectacular pythons is the rainforest-dwelling Green Tree Python (*Morelia viridis*). Juveniles are bright yellow; The plucky Frilled Lizard (*Chlamydosaurus kingii*) bluffs would-be attackers by puffing up its umbrella-like frill.

CROCODILES, TURTLES, SKINKS, geckoes, monitor lizards, legless lizards and approximately 188 snake species, including both venomous and non-venomous species, are found in Australia. Australia's largest reptile (and also the largest in the world) is the formidable Estuarine Crocodile (*Crocodylus porosus*), which may grow up to 7 m in length. One of the smallest reptiles in Australia is the Top End Dwarf Skink (*Menetia alanae*), which is fully grown at just 7 cm.

CAMP-LOVING LIZARDS

Monitor lizards, which are often known as goannas in Australia, are frequent and greedy reptilian visitors to campsites. They can wreak havoc by getting into foodstuffs, crawling into tents and chasing frightened campers. Australia has 26 species of these large lizards, which are known as monitor lizards because they stand on their back legs to "monitor" their surroundings. They can grow to 2 m long but, despite their fearsome appearance, their hissing threats are mostly bravado and they usually scurry off and climb a tree if their threats are ignored.

Left: Monitor lizards are thought to have evolved 90 million years ago.

A BAD REPUTATION

Most people know Australia has more venomous snakes than any other place on Earth, but that does not mean all snakes found here are deadly, far from it. Australia also has six harmless colubrid snakes and many harmless python species, which kill their prey by asphyxiation not venom. Of the continent's venomous snakes, very few live in highly populated areas and some have not yet been known to cause any fatalities. Despite an abundance of dangerous snakes, Australia has a relatively low annual snakebite death rate, which is largely due to the availability of effective antivenom. Australian hospitals are equipped with venom detection kits and by swabbing the bite doctors are able to identify the species and administer the appropriate antivenom.

the FACTS!

MOST REPTILES (apart from crocodiles) have a three-chambered heart that is more primitive and in some respects less efficient than the four-chambered hearts of crocodiles, birds and mammals.

GECKOES HAVE REMARKABLE feet that enable them to cling to vertical or upside-down surfaces. Beneath a gecko's toes are adhesive pads covered with millions of microscopic, tightly packed hair-like structures called setae. A weak molecular attractive force, known as van der Waals force, exists between the setae and the surface the gecko is walking on, allowing the gecko to "stick" to the wall or ceiling.

SNAKES HAVE ONLY ONE functional lung that can measure over two-thirds of their body length.

IN 2007, scientists at the University of Canberra found that heat can make male Central Bearded Dragons (*Pogona vitticeps*) change sex in the shell to hatch as females — incredibly, temperature can override the species' genetic sex.

THE FITZROY RIVER TURTLE (*Rheodytes leukops*) is known as the "bum-breathing turtle" because it obtains much of its oxygen from the water through its cloacal opening. It pumps water in and out of its bum up to 60 times a minute!

THE VENOMOUS Desert Death Adder (*Acanthophis pyrrhus,* below) cunningly uses its wriggling white tail tip to lure curious prey closer so it can strike and swallow it whole.

Above: The Southern Cassowary can become aggressive if competing for food or if at risk. It has powerful legs with long claws and is known to have killed two people in Australia.

Deadly & dangerous Australians

Australia's many animals capable of maiming or wounding humans are often a source of fascination or fear for overseas travellers. However, it must be remembered that the animals are only using features that nature has equipped them with for their own survival.

the FACTS!

IN 1905, a man who had been bitten by a snake drank one and a half bottles of whiskey on the 27 km drive to the doctor. On arrival, he was comatose and never regained consciousness. The doctor said that he probably would have survived the snake's bite, but not the bite of the whiskey!

SEVERAL PEOPLE in Australia have died from an allergic reaction to the bite of the Giant Bull Ant (*Myrmecia brevinoda*).

THE CANE TOAD (*Rhinella marina*) is an introduced species that produces venom in a gland behind the eye. The venom can cause serious illness in humans if it is ingested and has killed many thousands of native animals.

UNLIKE FOR MANY SPECIES, the male Sydney Funnel-web Spider (*Atrax robustus*) is far more dangerous than the female of the species. The male's venom is five times stronger than the female's.

DANGEROUS ANIMALS are those capable of wounding a person, but not of killing them outright. Some even seem fairly innocuous — and usually are unless provoked. Deadly animals are those that can strike with fatal intent and are known to have been responsible for human deaths.

In Australia, the most well-known deadly animals are crocodiles, snakes, spiders and sharks, but even the iconic kangaroo can be dangerous and, in rare circumstances, can even be deadly if it feels threatened. Some of the less likely animals that have inflicted fatal wounds include the Red Kangaroo (*Macropus rufus*), the Dingo (*Canis lupus dingo*), the Southern Cassowary (*Casuarius casuarius*) and the Swamp Buffalo (*Bubalus bubalis*).

Despite the threat of death from the more fearsome creepy crawlies and venomous animals, most people do not realise that statistically they are more at risk of dying from an allergy to a bee or wasp sting, than from a snakebite. The world's deadliest animal, in terms of human deaths, is probably the humble mosquito. This insect is responsible for the spread of debilitating diseases such as dengue fever and malaria, which claim millions of lives worldwide each year.

Inset, top: Scorpions found in Australia belong to the genus *Liocheles* and are not deadly, but their weak venom can cause pain for 15–45 minutes.

Above, top to bottom: The Western Taipan (*Oxyuranus microlepidotus*) is the most venomous snake on the planet but lives in isolated areas and has not been responsible for any deaths; The Eastern Brown Snake (*Pseudonaja textilis*) has caused more than half of Australia's total snakebite deaths.

THE FATAL FUNNEL-WEB

The Sydney Funnel-web (*Atrax robustus,* left) is the deadliest known spider in the world. As its name suggests, it is found around Sydney and on the central and northern coasts of New South Wales in places like Nowra, Lithgow and Newcastle. Strangely, the spiders on Sydney's north shore are twice as venomous as those found in other locations. Males, at just 2.5 cm, are smaller than females, which grow to more than 3.5 cm. Thirteen people are known to have perished after a bite from the Sydney Funnel-web since 1927. In 1980, an antivenom was produced and there have been no further deaths from this spider. Strangely, domestic pets seem to be less affected by the Sydney Funnel-web's venom and many have survived bites without antivenom.

Left to right: Box Jelly (*Chironex fleckeri*); Cone shell (*Conus* sp.); The venomous spines of the cleverly camouflaged Reef Stonefish (*Synanceia verrucosa*), the world's deadliest fish, cause agonising pain and even death.

DEATH FROM BELOW

Both the Irukandji (*Carukia barnesi*) and Box Jelly (*Chironex fleckeri*) are found in Australian waters, but because they are transparent they are rarely seen before they carry out their deadly stings. The Box Jelly has the most fast-acting venom known to man and has killed at least 60 people in Australia. The Irukandji has killed two people in Australia, but the effects of its venom take longer to be felt.

MIGHTY WHITE

The White Shark (*Carcharodon carcharias*) is sometimes also known as the Great White or White Pointer and is one of the most feared beasts in the world. It is responsible for almost half of the world's "unprovoked" shark attack deaths and inhabits tropical and temperate waters around the globe. Most attacks in Australia occur about 200 m from shore during November to March, which is when humans and sharks most often share the water. The White Shark is unique among sharks because it has flexible jaws that enable it to "chew" flesh off large prey, such as whales. It also has a special way of moving blood through its body to keep its body temperature warmer than that of the surrounding water and, for this reason, can swim faster and further than other sharks. It is a formidable predator with razor-sharp teeth, the outermost rows of which are shed and replaced as needed.

Above, top to bottom: Estuarine Crocodiles (*Crocodylus porosus*) are powerful predators famous for the violent "death roll" they use to kill their prey; The Blue-ringed Octopus (*Hapalochlaena maculosa*) is one of seven blue-ringed octopus species in Australia.

Below: Most research indicates that the White Shark grows only to around 7 m, despite speculation it can grow bigger. It has been seen lunging its enormous body out of the water to keep grasp of its prey.

the FACTS!

CONE SHELLS in the genus *Conus* are marine snails that, if disturbed, shoot a "harpoon-like" proboscis (mouthpiece) out and inject their harasser with venom. Geography Cone Shells (*Conus geographus*) have caused at least twelve deaths.

DEADLY blue-ringed octopuses can change colour to blend in to their background and, if threatened, vivid blue rings or patches break out on the body as a warning signal. A single blue-ringed octopus may contain enough venom to paralyse more than ten adult humans within minutes. The first fatality from the blue-ringed octopus was recorded in 1956 and at least two people are known to have died in Australia. Victims can die very quickly from lack of oxygen caused by paralysis. There is no antivenom and the only first aid treatment is to perform CPR (cardiopulmonary resuscitation).

FLYING-FOXES can carry a deadly disease known as lyssavirus and should never be handled by humans who are not wearing thick gloves.

DINGOES in the wild are mostly cautious and prefer to keep out of the way of humans. But some areas (such as Fraser Island, Qld, where Dingoes and humans come into contact) remind us they are wild animals and should never be fed or approached. Two confirmed fatal Dingo attacks have been made on humans, one of which occurred on Fraser Island in 2001.

POISONOUS OR TOXIC animals can also be deadly if eaten. Tetrodoxin, one of the most powerful poisons on Earth, is found in the skin and organs of pufferfish and has caused human deaths. Some species of crab also contain a poison called saxitoxin, and large reef fish can accumulate a poison called ciguatoxin, which causes ciguatera poisoning.

Above: The critically endangered Orange-bellied Parrot (*Neophyma chrysogaster*). Numbers were as low as just 30 individuals in the 1980s — today, 150–400 remain in the wild.

Endangered
Australians

For a country with just over 200 years of European occupation, Australia has an appalling record of extinctions. More than 50 native animal species and 60 species of plant have become extinct in Australia since 1788 and many more are endangered and need our help to survive.

MAMMALS HAVE SUFFERED the most, largely due to the introduction of non-native carnivores such as cats, foxes and dogs (which prey on native species), as well as competition for food with introduced rabbits, cows and sheep. The last mammal extinction was that of the Thylacine in the 1930s. Many birds, too, are on the endangered list and some, such as the Night Parrot, may be already extinct. Habitat destruction is the biggest threat faced by endangered species.

Above: Illegal trapping probably led to the decline of the endangered Gouldian Finch (*Erythrura gouldiae*), which once existed in large flocks in the NT. Although endangered in the wild, many keep it as an aviary bird.

the FACTS!

IN 1953, a schoolboy chanced across a remarkable discovery — the Western Swamp Turtle (*Pseudemydura umbrina*), which was believed extinct. They are still critically endangered inhabitants of seasonally dry swamps and are slow breeders that do not reach maturity until about fifteen years of age.

MELBOURNE ZOO'S last surviving Sharp-snouted Day-frog (*Taudactylus acutirostris*) died in 1995, which is alarming because the species may well be extinct in the wild. Thankfully, James Cook University, Queensland, also has live individuals.

BILBIES became extinct in South Australia in the 1930s, but, since 1995, Monarto Zoological Park in partnership with the Department of Environment and Heritage has been breeding a captive population.

Above, left to right: Vanishing frogs are an early warning for ecosystems and many are under threat. Captive breeding programs are underway at Taronga Zoo, NSW, to save the Southern Corroboree Frog (*Pseudophryne corroboree*); The Lord Howe Island Stick Insect (*Dryococelus australis*) was believed extinct until a single breeding pair was discovered in 2001. The female "Eve" gave birth to 250 young, which pulled this critically endangered insect back from the brink.

Above: A captive breeding program for the endangered Golden Bandicoot (*Isoodon auratus*) has been established in the Northern Territory. The species was only found in the Territory in 1994.

AUSTRALIA'S EASTER "BUNNY"

The Greater Bilby (*Macrotis lagotis*) is the largest member of the bandicoot family. It lives in arid, sandy areas of Australia, where it digs a cool underground burrow and is active mostly at night when the temperature drops. Its long, thin ears also help it stay cool, as blood circulating close to the ear's surface is cooled. Foxes, Dingoes, feral cats and competition with rabbits are affecting this small mammal's survival. Its cause has been taken up by the Save the Bilby Foundation and it has become Australia's version of the Easter Bunny. Unfortunately, the smaller Lesser Bilby is already extinct.

Right: The endangered Greater Bilby.

Conservation Watch

The Whale Shark (*Rhincodon typus*, far left) is the world's largest fish. Millions of people have visited Ningaloo Reef, WA, to swim with these gentle behemoths of the sea, which only eat krill.

FIGHT FOR THEM
ON THE BEACHES

All six species of marine turtle found in Australia are considered threatened with extinction. The 500 kg Leatherback Turtle (*Dermochelys coriacea*) is one of the most at risk and is an endangered visitor to Australia's eastern, northern and western coasts. Although they mostly nest overseas, some are known to come ashore near Bundaberg, Queensland, to lay eggs. Drowning in fishing nets and being struck by boat propellers, as well as having its eggs or hatchlings eaten by Dingoes, birds, goannas and feral pigs, are its major threats. They are also known to choke on plastic bags and litter that resembles sea jellies, which comprise most of their diet.

Below: Research and conservation programs are underway to help save these amazing, long-distance swimmers.

Below: Gilbert's Potoroo (*Potorous gilbertii*) is critically endangered. It too was thought to be extinct until rediscovered at Two People's Bay, WA. Only around 30 survive in the wild.

Above: Considered extinct until 1973, there are now fewer than 1000 Bridled Nailtail Wallabies (*Onychogalea fraenata*) found in the wild. Currently listed as endangered, it is part of captive breeding programs for reintroduction into the wild.

Above: For a long time it was thought that the endangered Pygmy Blue-tongue Lizard (*Tiliqua adelaidensis*) was extinct, until herpetologists discovered the remains of one of these lizards inside the stomach of a brown snake in 1994.

Above: The Swift Parrot (*Lathamus discolor*) is also endangered and is one of Australia's rare "migratory" parrot species. It breeds only in Tasmania but moves north to NSW and Victoria in winter.

the FACTS!

IN 1994, THE SOUTHERN OCEAN between Australia and Antarctica became a whale sanctuary that links up with another sanctuary established in the Indian Ocean in 1979. Sadly, Japan refuses to accept the sanctuary and continues to hunt whales (above left) in the Southern Ocean. Japan is estimated to have killed more than 21,000 whales since 1986.

INCREDIBLY, FEMALE MARINE TURTLES return to the beach of their birth to lay their eggs, sometimes making a journey of many thousands of kilometres.

OVER THE LAST DECADE ALONE, some schools of Orange Roughy (*Hoplostethus atlanticus*) have declined to just 10% of their original size. Despite this, Orange Roughy are still being fished — using unsustainable trawl-fishing methods that also catch "bycatch" such as Australian Fur-seals. Even today, Orange Roughy fillets continue to be sold in fish and chip shops around Australia.

LORD HOWE WOODHENS were once so plentiful that they were caught and eaten in huge numbers when Europeans first landed on Lord Howe Island. Now they are one of the rarest birds in the world.

THE ENDANGERED WOMA (*Aspidites ramsayi,* below) feeds on other snakes and has some immunity to the venom of King Brown Snakes (*Pseudechis australis*).

A wealth
of habitats

Above: Seemingly barren deserts support wildflowers, hardy shrubs and many reptile species.

the FACTS!

A TINY 6% of the continent is considered arable agricultural land.

COASTAL HEATH and mangrove walks around Australia introduce nature-lovers to native plant life, reptiles and birds.

DRY SCHLEROPHYLL FOREST, which covers much of Australia's arable land, is loosely termed "bush". The phrase comes from the Dutch word *bosch*, which was used to describe South African scrublands and was later taken up by the British.

AUSTRALIA'S ACACIA woodlands and tropical savanna grasslands rely on seasonal regimes of fire to help dormant seeds germinate.

MANGROVE HABITATS (below) are vital "nurseries" for many marine fish and crustaceans.

The continent's plant and animal life has been shaped by the diverse habitats that make up the Australian landscape. Animals and plants have evolved gradually over time to fill ecological niches or to better suit sometimes harsh and inhospitable conditions.

ALL AUSTRALIAN HABITATS, even highly saline salt lakes, freezing mountain tops and waterless deserts are utilised by specially adapted fauna and flora. The majority of the continent is covered by desert grasslands and acacia and Mulga woodlands, but vast swathes of coastal regions are furnished with more forgiving monsoon or tropical woodlands, coastal heath and wet and dry schlerophyll forest. All habitats are rich with wildlife and even the desert comes alive by night with nocturnal animals, many of which burrow into the cooler earth by day. On the extreme salt lakes, rare algae and lichen grow, and a variety of salt-tolerant fish attract birdlife such as Australian Pelicans and White-bellied Sea-Eagles.

Above, top to bottom: Marine invertebrates, sea birds, sea mammals and fish inhabit shallow inshore waters and beaches; Salt lakes support a surprising variety of life forms.

ALPINE-LOVING PYGMIES

Many tourists do not realise that Australia has snowy regions capable of supporting a snow-skiing industry in winter. These areas are also home to cold-adapted plants and animals that thrive in the freezing conditions. Australian Snow Gums and Snow Daisies dot the mountain sides and the tiny Mountain Pygmy-possum (*Burramys parvus*, bottom right) is a classic example of an animal that has evolved to make the most of these frigid environmental conditions. It hibernates under the windblown, snow-covered mountain scrub during winter, feeding on a cache of seeds and fruits it has collected over summer. Unfortunately, its limited habitat is being affected by climate change, threatening its existence.

Floral
magnificence

Like Australia's fauna, the continent's plant life has developed in isolation, leading to Australia having more unique plant species than any other country. Pockets of relict rainforest from Gondwanan times have also preserved species.

AUSTRALIA'S MOST COMMON

species are hardy acacias, eucalypts (of which Australia has more than 700 native species), grevilleas (the most commonly cultivated native plants), melalcucas (paperbarks) and eremophilas (emu bushes). Australia is also blessed with a kaleidoscopic array of wildflowers, including orchids, sundews and waratahs.

FLORA TO WATCH OUT FOR

Six stinging-trees in the *Dendrocnide* genus exist in Australia and are among the most dangerous ever found. Plants such as the Gympie-Gympie are covered with thin hairs that puncture the skin like needles and inject their very painful toxin.

JOSEPHINE'S GARDEN

French botanists collected specimens of Australian flora on exploratory missions, prompting Josephine, the wife of Emperor Napoleon, to grow more than 100 species of Australian plants including grevilleas, banksias, eucalypts and casuarinas at Malmaison, outside of Paris, France.

Above, left to right: The exquisite King Orchid (*Dendrobium kingianum*); Finke River Mallee (*Eucalyptus sessilis*); Scarlet Banksia (*Banksia coccinea*); Bottle Tree (*Brachychiton rupestris*).

A NATIVE LARDER & FIRST AID KIT

Aborigines used native plants as food, medicine, and to create materials such as dillybags. Burrawang (*Macrozamia communis,* below left) is an ancient plant that has been used by Aborigines for more than 13,000 years. Seeds bearing the plant's toxic fruit were soaked in running water for up to a week, then roasted in hot coals. Aborigines

ground up nardoo plants into a flour and ate the fruit of the Quandong (*Santalum acuminatum*). The Bunya Pine (*Araucaria bidwilli,* left) produces large cones containing protein-rich nuts. Annually, as many as 700 Aborigines from tribes throughout South-East Queensland congregated in Bunya Mountains National Park to feast on the bounty of the Bunya and engage in corroborees and ceremonies. Sugar was obtained from the nectar of the Yellow Flame Grevillea, which

Aborigines called "sugar bag". Top End Aborigines also developed several uses for Swamp Banksia (*Banksia dentata*). They mixed the nectar with water to make a sweet drink and smeared cones with animal fat to create torches that could be set alight. Old cones were even used as hairbrushes or to filter muddy water. The narcotic Pitjuri (*Duboisia hopwoodii*) and other plants were used as stimulants and species of native mint in the genus *Mentha* were used to cure coughs. Gum tree sap, which is rich in tannins, was rubbed on burns.

the FACTS!

JOSEPH BANKS came up with the name gum tree in 1770 when he found a tree that had gum exudations. Some gums were also known as "dragon trees".

AUSTRALIA'S MAJESTIC Antarctic Beech trees are descended from trees that pollen samples have shown existed more than 66 million years ago.

AUSTRALIA'S *Macrozamia lucida* cycad uses hot and smelly tactics to force tiny insects called thrips to help it pollinate. For one month of the year, male plants use conserved energy to raise the temperature of their tightly packed cones by more than 12°C. The heat increases the cones' pungent odour, caused by a chemical called beta-myrcene, and forces the thrips out. This means the temporarily evicted thrips are likely to visit the far less stinky female cycads during this time, thus pollinating the plants.

THERE ARE BETWEEN 1200–1350 species of wattle (*Acacia*) worldwide. They comprise Australia's largest flowering plant genus with 954 species.

BEAUTIFUL BLUE LECHENAULTIA (*Lechenaultia biloba*) grows so prolifically in some parts of South-West Western Australia that Aborigines referred to it as "the floor of the sky".

IN FINKE GORGE NATIONAL PARK, Red Cabbage Palms (*Livistona mariae*) are relics from Australia's ancient wetter days.

New South Wales
— the premier State

Above: The Scenic Cableway provides views over the Blue Mountains.

the FACTS!

THE FIRST EUROPEAN to step on shore in New South Wales was Isaac Smith on 29 April 1770.

THE FIRST HOUSE BUILT in Sydney was Governor Phillip's £130 pre-fabricated home, built three weeks after the First Fleet's arrival. It was on the corner of George and Bridge Streets but soon fell down as it was not wind and waterproof as its makers promised.

THE MOTTO OF THE STATE of New South Wales is *Orta recens quam pura nites* (Newly arisen, how brightly you shine).

IN 1805, approximately two-thirds of the children born in the colony of New South Wales were illegitimate (born out of wedlock).

SCOTTISH GOVERNOR Lachlan Macquarie, who governed the colony of New South Wales from 1810–1822, is often called the "Father of Australia" because of his extensive public works program.

IN 1890, THE PLAGUE ravaged the population of Sydney. It paved the way for social health reforms such as health and safety regulations and codes for the construction of buildings, water, sewage and drainage.

THE LAUGHING KOOKABURRA (*Dacelo novaeguineae*) is the State's avian emblem and the Platypus (*Ornithorhynchus anatinus*) is the faunal emblem.

New South Wales was the first State established and is the fourth-largest, with an area of 801,600 km² (which still makes it seven times bigger than England). More than half of the State's population lives in Sydney, the capital of New South Wales.

SYDNEY CENTRES ON THE DEEP, sapphire-blue harbour, which has been described as "the finest harbour in the world" and is considered the city's crowning jewel. Sydney Harbour, or Port Jackson as it is more correctly known, was not the first site chosen for a new British penal colony. Governor Arthur Phillip, who captained the First Fleet in 1788, deemed it superior to Botany Bay, the original choice. Thus, Sydney Cove became the birthplace of Australia and the State of New South Wales. The colonial past of New South Wales means that the State was once much larger than it is now. This is because Governor Phillip originally set the limits of the colony to include the entire eastern half of the continent, from Cape York to the bottom of Tasmania and "all the country inland, westward" from around Milingimbi (now in the Northern Territory) to Elliston, South Australia. Today, the State's northern boundary extends to Tweed Heads on the northern New South Wales coast, Albury on the border of Victoria, and Broken Hill on the border of South Australia.

THE RAT RACE

Today's Sydney is Australia's most populous, wealthy and progressive city. In fact, many Australians consider Sydney to be such a dynamic powerhouse for business and enterprise that the city's busy, always-on-the-go lifestyle is referred to as "the rat race". However, it is also a city that enjoys a stretch of beautiful beaches on its doorstep, and is surrounded by some of the most magnificent national parks. Thus, there are plenty of opportunities for residents to throw off their workaday worries and hit the beach or the holistic retreats of the nearby Blue Mountains.

Above, top to bottom: A replica tall ship sails towards the Opera House of today's Sydney — a reminder of the city's growth since the First Fleet dropped anchor in 1788; Sydneysiders flock to the water's edge for respite from the Summer heat.

Below: The impressive, futuristic-looking landmark of Centrepoint Tower is visible from many positions within the city.

REGIONAL BEAUTY

The larger cities of Sydney, Newcastle and Wollongong aside, New South Wales also boasts idyllic seaside retreats up and down the coast. In the south is the aptly named Eden; up north, the historic Port Macquarie, cosmopolitan Coffs Harbour and bohemian Byron Bay (above left) delight both tourists and locals. Inland, much of the State is prime grazing land, where large sheep and cattle farms compete with grain production for a share of the spoils. Major towns such as Tamworth, Armidale, Bathurst, Wagga Wagga and Dubbo have their own distinct character. Attractions include the annual Tamworth Country Music Festival, Armidale's vibrant university scene, and the excellent Western Plains Zoo at Dubbo.

HOME OF THE COOEE

The traditional yell of "Cooee" comes from the Dharug Aboriginal people who used it to communicate over long distances. The cry was later taken up by white Australians as a bushman's cry for help. In 1915, at the start of World War I, 35 men from Gilgandra in north-west New South Wales marched 500 km to Sydney in six weeks to enlist. They signalled their arrival with a "Cooee", and their effort became known as a "Cooee March"; hence, Gilgandra in New South Wales bills itself as the "Home of the Cooees".

WINE COUNTRY

The fertile viticultural region of the Hunter Valley (right), north-west of Newcastle, is the country's oldest wine-producing region and boasts some of the country's finest wines. Towns such as Cessnock, Pokolbin, Lovedale, Rothbury and Mount View attract those seeking a tipple, and boutique bed and breakfast accommodation set amid vineyards makes it a popular holiday destination.

SNOWY RIVER RIDERS

Elyne Mitchell's *The Silver Brumby* series and AB "Banjo" Paterson's famous poem *The Man from Snowy River* vividly recount the days when wild horses roamed Kosciuszko National Park in New South Wales and the Snowy Mountains across the Victorian border. The region around Cooma and Mt Kosciuszko is imbued with a rich sense of folklore inherited from the days of settlement when "all the tried and noted riders from the stations near and far … sent the flint stones flying" as they raced to catch brumbies "where the pine-clad ridges raise their torn and rugged battlements on high". The evocative vision of horses galloping free across snow-strewn mountains where the "air is clear as crystal, and the white stars fairly blaze at midnight" is certainly beautiful, but unfortunately, the brumbies have caused environmental damage to some of the State's most fragile habitats.

GOLD IN THE HILLS

The New South Wales town of Ophir is the place where gold was said to be first discovered in Australia in 1851. However, rumour has it that Government Surveyor James McBrien alerted authorities to alluvial gold near the Fish River, close to Bathurst, in 1823, and when WB Clarke revealed his find of gold near Lithgow in 1841 to Governor Gipps he was told, "Put it away … or we shall all have our throats cut". Because of the high number of criminals, gold was deemed to be a risky find until well after the Californian gold rush in the United States of America.

Above, left to right:
Byron Bay Lighthouse;
A horseman on Tom Groggins Station, NSW, evokes the "horsemen spirit";
The Waratah (*Telopea speciosissima*) is the State's floral emblem.

the FACTS!

FROM 1897 TO 1901, some people lived on top of Mt Kosciuszko, the nation's highest peak, manning a small weather station. One meteorologist even lived there for 27 months.

SYDNEY HAS SIX sister cities. They are Hampshire and Portsmouth in the UK, Nagoya in Japan, San Francisco in the USA, Wellington, NZ, and Guangzhou in China.

MANLY HOSTED the first official world surfing championship in 1964. It was won by "Midget" Farrelly.

THE WORLD'S HIGHEST free-standing pinnacle, 561-m-high Balls Pyramid on Lord Howe Island is within NSW territory. Businessman Dick Smith raised the State flag on its craggy summit in 1980. This rugged, knife-life rock is also home to the world's rarest insect, the Lord Howe Island Stick Insect.

LIGHTNING RIDGE, in the State's north-west, is one of the few places where rare black opals are found.

WINGEN, north-west of Newcastle, is aptly named after the Aboriginal word for fire. A burning coal seam, which is believed to have been lit by lightning, has been pouring sulphurous smoke through fissures on a nearby hill for more than 1000 years.

THE SMALL TOWN OF KIAMA, south of Wollongong, draws many thousands of tourists each year to witness an unusual coastal phenomenon. The Blowhole shoots a towering blast of water metres skyward with each surge of the tide.

Queensland
— the sunshine State

Above: Brisbane is Australia's fastest-growing capital city.

the FACTS!

EUROPEANS FIRST LAID EYES on what is now the State of Queensland when Willem Jansz sighted land on western Cape York Peninsula in 1606. He and his crew gave Cape Keerweer (which means "turnabout") the country's first European place name.

POSSESSION ISLAND, QLD, where Cook first proclaimed the east coast as British land, was later found, by JT Embley, to have rich quartz reefs of gold in 1895. Cook and his men had not noticed it when they stood on the spot in August 1770. If they had, Australia's pattern of settlement might have been very different.

WHEN JOHN OXLEY explored Moreton Bay in 1823, he discovered three escaped convicts — Thomas Pamphlett, Richard Parsons and John Finnegan — who led him to the mouth of the river on which the State capital, Brisbane, would later be established.

BRISBANE TOWN was only declared a city in 1902.

WHEN THE FIRST GOVERNOR of Queensland, Sir George Bowen, took up his tenure, he found he had a mere 7.5 pence in the treasury — within two days even that had been stolen!

SURFERS PARADISE on the Gold Coast probably would not be half as popular had it kept its original name of Elston!

Right: Aussies and visitors soak up the rays on the Gold Coast.

Queensland is the second-biggest Australian State and has an area of 1,730,648 km². Its balmy tropical climate and seemingly endless sunshine make it a popular holiday State.

QUEENSLAND'S CAPITAL CITY, Brisbane, has often been described as a big country town, but recent growth has seen it flourish as a contemporary yet laidback city with all the attractions expected of an international tourist destination. It was established in 1824 as a penal colony, and was regarded as one of the most depraved places of torment under the command of Captain Patrick Logan. Today, Brisbane bears little physical evidence of its convict past and only two buildings survive from its early days — the Old Mill on Wickham Terrace and the Commissariat Store in William Street. Understandably, Queensland's natural environments are often more of a drawcard than its towns. The State's coastal landscape is magnificent, with golden beaches enhanced by the wonder of the Great Barrier Reef in the north. Much of the hinterland is subtropical forest or rainforest, or arable farming lands beyond which are the Great Dividing Range and the outback's river flats and rolling semi-arid grasslands and woodlands. The north of the State has two seasons — the Wet and the Dry — but the South-East Corner is usually mild for most of the year, with pleasantly warm winters and summer sunshine.

Above: The bougainvillea-festooned arbour of South Bank, which was once the scene for the 1988 World Expo but is now a vibrant leisure hub for Brisbane city.

COASTS TO BOAST ABOUT

Queensland lays claim to some of the country's most exclusive and cosmopolitan beachside resort strips, including the Gold Coast, Sunshine Coast, Discovery Coast and the Whitsunday Islands. Closest to Brisbane is the "glitter strip" of the Gold Coast, where the white-sand beaches are fringed with high-rises, and numerous exclusive boutiques and shopping centres cater for affluent travellers. About two hours north of Brisbane, the languid, family-oriented beaches of the more relaxed "Sunny Coast", entice families and backpackers, with Noosa alone having garnered a reputation as a playground for the jet-set. Further north, the Discovery Coast is a must for campers looking to escape civilisation and soak up the vibe of tiny holiday towns with little to offer but friendly locals and beautiful views. In the State's north, the idyllic Whitsunday Islands and the lure of the Reef, which stretches all the way up to the tourist haven of Cairns, draw sunseekers and thrillseekers.

Queensland Critters

The Brolga (*Grus rubicunda*) and the Koala (*Phascolarctos cinereus*) are the respective avian and faunal emblems of Queensland.

HEROINE OR STORYTELLER?

Fraser Island, Queensland, is named after Mrs Eliza Fraser (left), who survived the shipwreck of the *Stirling Castle* in 1836 only to confound the public with various stories about her ordeal. She claimed Aborigines had captured her and her husband, Captain Fraser, stolen their clothes, treated them like slaves and killed her husband and the first and second mates when they became too weak to work. There is no doubt that when found wandering in Moreton Bay, she was "perfectly black … dreadfully crippled … and a mere skeleton" — in the words of Lieutenant Charles Otter. She soon became a celebrated "brave white woman". If what she claimed was true, it was no more than what many Aborigines had suffered at the hands of whites, but her story later did not correspond with that given by local Aborigines and changed dramatically over several tellings. She undoubtedly suffered, including the death of her husband, but we may never know the truth. She eventually died in an English mental asylum.

Above: The Esplanade, Cairns, Qld.

the FACTS!

THE STATE MOTTO on Queensland's Coat of Arms is *Audax at fidelis*, which translates as "bold, aye, but faithful too".

STRANGELY, QLD'S Coat of Arms includes three introduced animals — a Red Deer, a bull and a ram — which signify the pastoral industry. The only Australian animal on the shield is the Brolga.

IN *PORTRAIT OF BRISBANE*, writer Bill Scott described the city as "a lazy town with its sleeves rolled up, casually sprawling across its thirty-seven hills".

IN A COUNTRY that sparked the Rum Rebellion, rum was always going to be a popular product. The Australian-made Bundaberg Rum (affectionately known as "Bundy") is produced from sugar harvested near Bundaberg, Queensland, and is a popular spirit that will, according to an old ditty, "tan your insides and grow hair on your bum".

THE COOKTOWN ORCHID is Queensland's floral emblem. Cooktown, where Cook and his crew camped while they fixed the *Endeavour* in 1770, contains no fewer than six monuments to the navigator.

CAPITAL OF THE NORTH

North Queenslanders at one time considered that they should be granted a separate State to the rest of Queensland, and Townsville was proposed as the likely capital of the north. During World War II, the division was exacerbated when Labor politician Eddie Ward leaked plans of a supposed "Brisbane Line" — an imaginery line above Brisbane, beyond which troops would retreat to protect the capital and the populous south-east of the continent in the event of a Japanese land invasion, leaving the north to fend for itself. Even today, some north Queenslanders treat "townies" from the South-East with derision.

LIVING IN PARADISE

Few people have the luxury of living their lives on a bountiful tropical island, but naturalist Ted Banfield and his wife, along with their housekeeper Essie McDonough, did just that. They were able to lease, then later own, Dunk Island (right) for 26 years before Ted died, aged 70, in 1923. He published many books on his idyllic lifestyle, including the best-selling *Confessions of a Beachcomber* in 1908.

GO WEST!

"Beach meets bush" could be one way to sum up Queensland, because the western half of the State is true country territory, where the fertile grazing lands of the Darling Downs give way to the cattle country of Roma, Longreach, Rockhampton and Charters Towers and the rough and tumble mining towns of "The Isa" (Mount Isa) and Cloncurry.

CAIRNS INTERNATIONAL

The proximity of Cairns to the world-renowned natural wonders of the Daintree Rainforest and the Reef have made it a popular destination for both domestic and international visitors, attracting millions of visitors annually.

Northern Territory
— the great escape

the FACTS!

THE NORTHERN TERRITORY'S Coat of Arms fittingly includes more Aboriginal elements than any other coat of arms, including an Aboriginal ritual stone or *Tjurunga* and an Arnhem Land rock painting. Its flag (top) is also very distinctive and original, featuring the colours of black, white and red ochre with a symbolised Sturt's Desert Rose (left).

DESPITE HAVING an Australian city named after him, Charles Darwin had few nice things to say about the continent. He wrote in his diary on 14 March 1836, "You are a rising child, and doubtless some day will reign a great princess of the South: but you are too great and ambitious for affection, yet not great enough for respect. I leave your shores without sorrow or regret".

THE NORTHERN PART of the Territory, known as the Top End, receives wet season monsoonal weather for three to five months annually. The bottom half of the Territory has no rivers and receives little rainfall.

The Northern Territory was initially part of New South Wales and then part of South Australia until 1911 when the Commonwealth resumed control. It was granted self government only in 1978.

AT 1,346,200 KM², the Territory makes up one-sixth of the continent's land mass and is true outback country. A number of unsuccessful settlements were made in the Northern Territory prior to the establishment of Darwin, then called Palmerston, in 1869. The first was Port Essington in 1824. Most of the settlements failed because they were not on established trade routes, were extremely isolated and were frequently attacked by Aborigines. The isolation means that, even today, almost half of the Territory's residents live in the capital, Darwin; the rest are scattered in smaller regional towns, such as Katherine, Gove, and Alice Springs or live on vast, remote cattle stations or in Aboriginal communities. Aboriginal people make up a large percentage of the population and Darwin is proudly multicultural with a large Chinese, Greek and South-East Asian population.

THE LIGHT FANTASTIC

The port on Fannie Bay was named "Port Darwin" by John Lort Stokes, the captain of the HMS *Beagle*, after his crewmate Charles Darwin — the famous evolutionary biologist. When a group of Aboriginal warriors came upon members of the HMS *Beagle* close to where the city of Darwin stands today, two men, LR Fitzmaurice and Charles Keys, began to dance and shout as a way to amuse the Aborigines and perhaps prevent them from attacking. The ploy worked and the men gambolled about for their curious audience until a boat landed nearby to rescue them. John Lort Stokes, the leader of the expedition, wrote, "No one could recall to mind, without laughing, the ludicrous figure necessarily cut by our ship-mates, when to amuse the natives, they figured on the light fantastic toe".

Above: Boats at their moorings in Darwin Harbour today, with the city's cyclone-proof, low-rise architecture beyond.

LASSETER'S LOST MINE

Seventeen-year-old prospector Harold Bell Lasseter claimed to have found a rich reef of gold in the Northern Territory in 1897, although the site was lost due to faulty instruments. Lasseter initiated another search for the missing gold in 1930, but the party became lost and failed. In November the same year, Lasseter set off alone but subsequently disappeared. His diary, which was found at his last campsite, records that he rediscovered the reef on 23 December, before he had turned for home, but did not say where. His camels bolted on his return journey and he died near Irving Creek. His rich reef of gold has never been found.

Symbolic Territorians
The regal Wedge-tailed Eagle
(*Aquila audax*) is the Territory's
avian emblem.

Above, left to right: Endemic Magpie
Geese flock to Kakadu's wetlands;
The Wedge-tailed Eagle.

CHRISTMAS TRAGEDY

On Christmas Day 1974, Darwin was battered by ferocious cyclone Tracy and winds of up to 217 km/h all but destroyed the town. Seventy-one people perished and hundreds more were injured. Approximately 90% of the town's buildings were destroyed by the cyclone and more than half the population had to be evacuated following the devastation. The city was rebuilt with strict building standards and now has many cyclone-proof buildings.

Above, top to bottom: Flora River Nature Park in the Top End; More than 1.3 million people visit the Northern Territory annually, many of them using Darwin or Alice Springs as a base to then drive through the famed Red Centre.

ABORIGINAL LAND

Large parts of the Northern Territory are Aboriginal land or are managed by traditional custodians. Aboriginal land includes much of the rugged Arnhem Land escarpment, where numerous ancient rock art galleries have been found, as well as Aboriginal artefacts such as stone axes, which are among the oldest found in Australia. In 1916, a 6216 km^2 cattle station at Oenpelli was purchased by the Northern Territory Administration and turned into an Aboriginal reserve in 1920. A mission was also established at Galiwinku, an island off Darwin, and became one of Arnhem Land's biggest Aboriginal communities.

A TOWN LIKE ALICE

The Territory's second-largest city, Alice Springs, is a natural tourist base for visiting the Red Centre, Uluru and the impressive Kings Canyon. In 1949, London-born Neville Shute Norway wrote *A Town Like Alice* after a visit to the isolated outback town 1500 km south of Darwin. The novel later made the town world famous when it was published in 1950, although it is largely a work of fiction.

A PLAN FOR JAPAN

In 1877, when the South Australian government controlled what is now the Northern Territory, they considered signing over part of the land to Japan. The reason given was to accelerate population growth and economic development in the north. The plan fell through only because Japanese Samurai warriors revolted in Satsuma against the modernisation of Japan. The Japanese Imperial troops had to be sent to quell the uprising (made famous in the movie *The Last Samurai*). Just sixty-five years later, the first Japanese bombs fell on Northern Territory soil during World War II.

the FACTS!

EXPLORER LUDWIG Leichhardt was the first European to traverse the inland of the Top End in 1844.

ON 19 FEBRUARY 1942, Darwin was bombed by 188 Japanese planes. Twenty-four aircraft and eight ships were destroyed and 253 people lost their lives in the attack.

IN THE EARLY DAYS of European settlement, governments paid a bounty for each Wedge-tailed Eagle killed by farmers, who believed the birds killed lambs. Around 12,500 bounties each year were paid before research showed that rabbits actually made up at least 90% of the Wedge-tailed Eagle's diet; thus, the birds were helping farmers rather than hindering them.

RUMOUR HAS IT that a policeman, with the lofty name of Cornelius Power, was bored with his post in the tiny Gulf town of Borroloola in the 1890s and wrote to the Carnegie Corporation in New York requesting they send some books to establish a library. The Corporation, unaware of the size of the town, sent an enormous library. However, the truth is that the Governor of Victoria supplied the books and in 1935 the library had just 1793 books.

DURING THE BATTLE of Britain in WWII, there was a proposal to rename the Northern Territory "Churchill's Land" to show allegiance with the British.

MELVILLE ISLAND, 25 km off the Northern Territory's coast, is Australia's second-biggest island (after Tasmania) and is home to the Tiwi people. Tiwi Islanders paint their faces and bodies with geometric shapes and construct elaborate funeral poles that range from 1–2.5 m in height.

Western Australia
— the biggest State

Above: Mitchell Falls plunge into a deep pool in WA's rugged Kimberley region.

The entire western third of the continent is taken up by Western Australia, the largest Australian State at 2,525,500 km² — about the same size as Western Europe.

WESTERN AUSTRALIA COMPRISES vast sandy deserts, stunning beaches, the mountainous Stirling, Hamersley and Kimberley ranges, and the lush, wildflower-strewn South-West, renowned for its wineries. For such a large State, it is sparsely populated, making up only around 9% of Australia's total population. Approximately three-quarters of the State's residents live in the capital city, Perth.

Above: Skyscrapers tower over Perth city. The city has few heritage buildings, giving it a contemporary vibe.

Perth was founded as the Swan River colony by Lieutenant-Governor James Stirling, in 1829. Nearby Fremantle was established by Captain Charles Fremantle earlier the same year. The colony was slow to flourish and convict labour was actively sought from 1850, after which the colony continued to receive convicts until 1868. Today, Perth is a strikingly modern capital that has prospered off the State's rich mining industry, which first boomed with the Coolgardie and Kalgoorlie gold rushes in the 1890s and then again in the 1960s with other minerals. Wealthy mining magnates give Perth the highest proportion of self-made millionaires per population in any of the world's cities. Natural gas, iron ore, bauxite, nickel and uranium mining are the backbone of the industry. The north is marked out by the rugged Kimberley and the coastal town of Broome. In the State's South-West, Margaret River is an acclaimed wine-growing region dotted with historic towns and spectacular national parks. Much of the inland is covered with desert and salt lakes.

Above: Brookland Estate Winery, Margaret River. The region is considered one of Australia's most popular viticulture regions and Margaret River wines are exported around the world.

Wild WA

The faunal emblems of Western Australia are the Numbat (*Myrmecobius fasciatus,* left) and Black Swan (*Cygnus atratus,* bottom).

IN BLOOM

More endemic flora is found in Western Australia than in any other Australian State. As much as 85% of the flora in the South-West Corner is found nowhere else. In 1961, the Brand government determined that road verges must be a minimum width to encourage the protection of the State's flora; as a result, a rich tapestry of colour adorns the roadsides and the native wildflowers flourish even in gravelly or sandy soils. Approximately 8000 native species have been recorded and a further 2000 likely new species are yet to be classified. Some of the most exquisite are the many delicate orchid species, such as the elegant Blue China Orchid.

DEATH OF A PEARLER

Broome, on Western Australia's north-west coast, has the largest Japanese cemetery in Australia on account of its history as a centre for pearling. Japanese pearl divers worked on pearling luggers from the late 1890s and the first interment in the cemetery is dated 1896. Hundreds of divers drowned or died of the dreaded "bends", a form of paralysis caused by surfacing too rapidly. Cyclones at sea also claimed the lives of many. Pearls (above), still contribute to WA's industry, with pearl farms found along the coast. Another unusual cemetery found in Western Australia is the Dog Cemetery at Corrigin, a wheatbelt town 225 km south-east of Perth. Strangely, the cemetery has become a popular tourist attraction and the shire's website explains that the "Dog Cemetery is a tribute to Man's Best Friend. With over 80 loved ones now buried, the cemetery is unique to Corrigin".

HUTT RIVER PROVINCE

Under a Unilateral Declaration of Independence, eccentric Leonard Casley turned his farm into his own "sovereign and independent province" in 1970 after falling out with the Commonwealth government over a wheat quota. He proclaimed himself Prince Leonard of the Hutt River Province (and his wife Princess Shirley) and the now "province" even has its own diplomatic passport that is accepted by France, Greece, Syria and The Vatican. Some 50,000 people visit the province annually to have their passports stamped and to buy some Hutt River Province currency.

A FATAL FEAT

Before engineer Charles Yelverton O'Connor began to construct a water pipeline to the Coolgardie and Kalgoorlie goldfields in 1898, water was such an expensive commodity on the goldfields that it cost more than champagne and was selling at around a dollar a litre. The pipeline scheme was nothing if not ambitious and was heavily opposed in parliament and deemed ludicrous. O'Connor, upset by the ongoing criticism, shot himself in March 1902, just four years into the project, leaving a suicide note that said, "The position has become impossible". He also left detailed instructions on how to complete the engineering project, which was finished on time and only a little over budget. It remains one of the greatest feats of engineering ever undertaken in Australia.

the FACTS!

WHEN MRS ALICE "Ninni" Watts threw a fish to a bottlenose dolphin from her husband's boat in 1964, she had little idea that she was starting a huge tourist attraction. The dolphin, nicknamed Charlie, returned the next day, and the next, and soon brought a small pod with him. The dolphins at Monkey Mia now draw huge crowds who wish to interact with these friendly sea mammals.

BERT "THE CHIEF" was an American who lived and worked at the isolated mining settlement of Gwalia, to Kalgoorlie's north, in 1898. He was well liked in the town, where he was said to have bathed in beer when no water was available and rode a camel when there was no other transport. Bert later returned to Australia in 1905 to manage the Bewick's mining operation before establishing his own mining company. He went on to become the 31st President of the United States of America — Herbert Clark Hoover — in 1928.

THE VALLEY OF THE GIANTS near Walpole-Nornalup National Park is home to rare stands of enormous Karri and Red Tingle trees. Four rare eucalypt species grow within this 4 km area. The Karri is the third-tallest tree known to man, after the Californian Redwood and the Australian Mountain Ash.

IN 1629, the ship *Batavia* was wrecked off the Houtman Abrolhos Islands near Geraldton. While the captain rowed for help, murderous crew members slaughtered the survivors in a grisly act of mutiny.

South Australia
— the festival State

the FACTS!

THE SOUTHERN HAIRY-NOSED Wombat (*Lasiorhinus latifrons,* above) is South Australia's faunal emblem. The State's floral emblem is Sturt's Desert Pea (*Swainsona formosa,* bottom).

SOUTH AUSTRALIA is so vast and dry that 80% of the State contains just 1% of the population. Most people live in Adelaide or on the Yorke, Fleurieu and Eyre Peninsulas.

SAILORS ABOARD the Dutch ship the *Gulden Zeepaard* were probably the first Europeans to see the South Australian coastline.

SOUTH AUSTRALIA does not have a motto on its State shield, just the words "South Australia".

A SMALL SURVEYING ERROR when defining the boundaries of South Australia in 1840 means that Victoria owns a 3.6-km-wide and 445-km-long sliver of what should be South Australia. The eastern border of South Australia was set at longitude 141 degrees east, but the portion that adjoins Victoria was actually drawn at 140°58'E. Over the years, the two States argued about this finger of land, and appealed to the Privy Council, but the border remained as it was drawn.

IN NOVEMBER 1876, a group of spiritualists in Adelaide swore they had been visited by the ghost of Colonel Light, who seemed particularly interested in warning them to fix the city's drainage problems to avoid an epidemic of yellow fever. It was thought to be a ploy to get the council to improve the sewerage system.

South Australia is the only State that shares a border with all other mainland States. With thirteen wine-producing regions and year-round cultural events it is little wonder it is known as the "festival State".

SOUTH AUSTRALIA is the third-largest State, covering 984,000 km². It is also the driest — four-fifths of it receive less than 254 mm of rain annually. The south-eastern corner, around the capital, Adelaide, is the most populous region. Adelaide is richly multicultural and hosts internationally renowned festivals such as WOMADelaide.

Above: Street performers and many annual festivals make Adelaide a vibrant city.

Above: Adelaide, on the Torrens River, was designed by Colonel William Light in 1838. He structured the city around a grid of wide, tree-lined streets, making Adelaide a spacious, well-planned city.

A CRIM'S CONCEPT

South Australia was the only mainland State that never accepted convicts. It was instead a "free State" that sold land to settlers to attract enterprise and skilled labour. Strangely, the idea of excluding convict labour in favour of paying settlers was devised by a prisoner! Edward Gibbon Wakefield, who suggested the plan in his famous *A Letter from Sydney*, had never been to Australia and was in gaol in Newgate Prison, England (for abducting a fifteen-year-old heiress) when he conceived the idea.

FREE BUT STARVING

The first South Australian settlers arrived on the HMS *Buffalo* on 28 December 1836 and landed where Glenelg stands today. Unfortunately, the land they had purchased sight unseen was not immediately available. It was only after Surveyor-General William Light began to survey the site for today's Adelaide that many settlers were able to take up the land they were promised. While they waited, they lived in hastily erected squats and had little means of growing food or making a living. Many were forced to eat native plants and wildlife, including crows, leading people in other States to label them "crow-eaters".

A MARREE MYSTERY

The largest work of art in the world was discovered near the town of Marree in 1998. Marree Man is a 4-km-long "geoglyph" (topological engraving) of an Aboriginal man and is so big it can only be appreciated from the air. Surveyors believe it was created by someone clearing the ground's surface of vegetation using a bulldozer following GPS directions, but its creator is unknown. In 2006, friends of eccentric Adelaide Hills artist Bardius Goldberg said they were sure the work was his, but its creator has never come forward. Goldberg died in 2002.

TEUTONIC PRISONERS

German, Silesian and Prussian Lutherans, most fleeing religious persecution, began to settle the free State of South Australia from the 1830s. Following the outbreak of World War I with Germany in 1914, Australians became suspicious of the Germans in their midst and about 6700 innocent Germans were imprisoned during the war years. Teaching German was banned in South Australian primary schools and 49 Lutheran schools were closed. Teutonic place names such as Lobethal, Blumberg, Hahndorf (above) and Klemzig were changed to Tweedvale, Birdwood, Ambleside and Gaza. Place names in other States were also changed. Most of the towns reverted to their German monikers after the 1930s.

LIFE UNDERGROUND

Coober Pedy, 850 km north of Adelaide is undoubtedly one of the strangest towns in the world. The town's name is said to be derived from the Aboriginal words *kupa piti,* which translate as "white man in a hole" — an apt name, because 80% of the white miners who live in the town do indeed live in "holes", or in cavernous, subterranean dugouts. Opal was discovered in Coober Pedy in 1915 and the town is now the self-proclaimed "Opal Capital of the World" and supplies about 70% of the world's demand. Returned servicemen moved to the town following the end of WWI and sought to escape the punishing 35–45°C summer heat by digging trenches (dugouts) similar to those they fought in during the war. Coober Pedy even has an underground bar, several churches and a subterranean art gallery.

FLINDERS HONOURS

Matthew Flinders circumnavigated Australia but was so humble he never named a single place after himself (Flinders Island, off South Australia, is named for his brother, Robert). However, his admirers later bestowed numerous South Australian places with his name, including Flinders Street, Flinders Chase Conservation Park, Flinders University and the magnificent Flinders Ranges (below).

Cool as a Cave Church

Gwyneth and Bill Ostling (left) are outback preachers from Coober Pedy's underground Catacombs Church.

Above: Huge swathes of the State are seasonally very dry and uninhabitable.

the FACTS!

THE TOWN OF GAWLER in the 1880s was known as a "colonial Athens" largely because of a strange "free-thinking" society known as the Humbug Society. It was set up by Jefferson Stowe and George Isaacs in 1859, rejected hypocrisy and sham, and was run by three officers — the amusingly titled Arch Flan, Bouncible Bam and Surprising Sham. Members met at the Globe Hotel, where new members had to buy a round of drinks for other members. In 1860, the Arch Flan EL Grundy even became an elected member for Gawler! The society published its own satirical newspaper, *The Bunyip,* which is still published today.

BLUE LAKE, near Mount Gambier, 486 km from Adelaide, nestles in the crater of an extinct volcano and undergoes an amazing colour change each year. Each November, the waters of the 77-m deep lake mysteriously change from grey to the deep blue for which it is named, remaining blue until March.

IN 1893, several reports of a "tiger" were made around the small South Australian town of Tantanoola. The animal was later shot in 1895 and turned out to be an Assyrian Wolf! Its stuffed body is on display at the Tantanoola Tiger Hotel.

Victoria
— the garden State

Victoria

Above: Melbourne is one of only two Australian cities (Adelaide is the other) that still uses trams.

the FACTS!

THE FIRST KNOWN Europeans on Victorian soil were survivors of the shipwrecked *Sydney Cove*, which ran aground on Preservation Island in 1797. They set out to walk to Sydney and the survivors were eventually rescued by fishermen.

JOHN BATMAN, one of the founders of Melbourne, was an interesting fellow. He married an escaped convict he had kept hidden for years and suggested Melbourne be named "Batmania". He contracted syphilis shortly after settling in Melbourne and was wheeled around the fledgling settlement in a pram until he died in May 1839.

THE MOTTO FOR MELBOURNE is *Vires acquirit eundo* (We gather strength as we grow).

VICTORIA'S STATE shield is held up by two women — one represents peace; the other prosperity.

OF ALL THE Australian States, Victoria was the first to have its own flag, a British Blue Ensign with the State badge and a crown above. The flag was first used in 1870.

ABORIGINAL GROUPS from around Victoria travelled to the Bogong High Plains in early summer to feast on the large, grey Bogong Moths, which sometimes numbered more than 14,000 per square metre. The migratory moths, which annually fly south from Queensland and New South Wales, were caught, crushed and roasted on hot coals.

FROM WWI TO 1966 (when the law was changed) Melbourne pubs had to close at 6 pm. The rush of workers heading to the pub for a drink as soon as they left work at 5 pm became known as the "six o'clock swill". Now Melbourne is renowned for its nightlife and cafe culture.

Although Victoria is the smallest mainland State, at just 227,600 km^2, it is also the most heavily populated. The capital, Melbourne, is situated on the banks of the Yarra River on Port Phillip Bay.

VICTORIA WAS ONE OF THE LAST STATES to be settled but its population was quickly enhanced by the gold rush and many prospectors stayed on to settle the fertile pastoral lands of the Western District. Because much of the southern area of the State is suited to agriculture, Victoria is sometimes also known as the "garden State". Of the rest of the State, more than 35% is forest and 12% is protected in national parks.

A GLITTERING CITY

More than 90% of all the gold found in Australia during the 1850s came from Victoria, where the country's richest gold rushes occurred. Much of the wealth was funnelled back into the elaborate enhancement of Melbourne city, which was variously known as Marvellous Melbourne, the Queen of the South and Smellbourne (when its cramped population started to pollute the streets and the Yarra with ever-increasing effluent).

During the extravagant days of the gold rush, some lucky fortune hunters were said to be so wealthy that, when in Marvellous Melbourne, they bathed in tubs of champagne and lit their pipes with banknotes.

HOME OF THE ARTS

Many people, particularly Melburnians, regard Melbourne as the cultural capital of Australia and it is true that many of Australia's most famous performing artists have hailed from Victoria. Melbourne is also the birthplace of Australia's film industry and the Salvation Army's *Soldiers of the Cross*, which screened in the Melbourne Town Hall in 1901, is considered the world's first "movie", closely followed by *The Story of the Kelly Gang* in 1907. The Australian Ballet School is located in Victoria's capital, and the Melbourne Theatre Company and Symphony Orchestra are both highly acclaimed. The National Gallery of Victoria also displays some of Australia's most significant artwork.

Below: City lights, fountains and public artwork grace the Southbank Promenade in Melbourne.

Symbols of the State

The Helmeted Honeyeater (*Lichenostomus melanops cassidix,* left) is the avian emblem and Common Heath (*Epacris impressa,* far left) is the floral emblem.

PHILLIP ISLAND'S PENGUIN PARADE

At Phillip Island, 140 km south-east of Melbourne, Little Penguins (*Eudyptula minor*) are the star attraction, especially when they conduct their daily waddling "parade" up Somerland Beach at sunset to return to their burrows. The island is also home to the second-largest colony of Australian Fur-seals, as well as the Koala Conservation Centre. The Phillip Island Motorcycle Grand Prix circuit and A Maze'N Things — a small theme park filled with optical illusions, mazes and puzzles — add to the fun.

PRIDE OF THE MURRAY

The Victorian town of Echuca on the Murray River was the second-largest port in the country during the 1870s. The wharf was more than 1 km long and was made of red gum. More than 100 boats plied the river during the 1870s and 1880s.

A SNOWY SCHEME

Following World War II, the ambitious Snowy Mountains Hydro-electric Scheme employed thousands of immigrants and locals for 25 years in a bid to trap the bountiful waters of the Snowy River before they flowed to the ocean in eastern Victoria. The water was diverted inland to irrigate land near the Murray and Murrumbidgee Rivers in Victoria and New South Wales, and used to generate hydro-electricity (supplying 10% of New South Wales' electricity needs). The scheme was a massive undertaking that required the construction of sixteen major dams, seven power stations, a pumping station and tunnels, pipelines and aqueducts extending 225 km. Remarkably, just 2% of the entire construction is visible above the ground.

LOVELY LAKES

The Lakes District in Gippsland comprises three large, shallow coastal lagoons that make up Australia's largest inland waterway system. The region is a birdwatcher's paradise, particularly Rotamah Island.

THE GREAT OCEAN ROAD

Victoria's Great Ocean Road, which stretches some 243 km from Torquay to Allansford, near Warrnambool, passes some of the most spectacular and rugged sea coast found in Australia, including the eroded "sea art" stacks (above) of Port Campbell National Park. Construction of the road began on 19 September 1919 and employed many ex-servicemen returning from World War I, who carved the road from thick rock using pickaxes and crowbars. The first stretch, a 75 km section between Anglesea and Apollo Bay, was completed by 1932. Quaint seaside towns along the way pay homage to the soldiers, with numerous WWI memorials. Lorne, Port Fairy, Apollo Bay and other tourist spots provide interesting diversions from the magnificent scenery. The world-renowned surf spot of Bells Beach is also found along the Great Ocean Road and in summer months Southern Right Whales may be seen frolicking in the ocean.

the FACTS!

VICTORIA'S FAUNAL EMBLEM is Leadbeater's Possum (*Gymnobelideus leadbeateri*, above). It has a very limited distribution of only around 100 km² near Marysville, to Melbourne's east, to Tanjil Bren. It was believed extinct in 1909 until it was found in 1961 at Marysville.

THE YARRA RIVER was known as the *Yarra Yarra* by Aborigines, which means "flowing water".

THE LARGEST EARTHWORM in the world is found in Victoria. It grows to an incredible 3.65 m long.

IN 1857, the secret ballot box, the symbol of Australian democracy, was devised in Victoria. Prior to this, those who were allowed to vote had to call out their choice.

WILSONS PROMONTORY (below) or "The Prom" as locals call it, is the southernmost point of the Australian mainland.

Tasmania
— the island State

Above: The charismatic Tassie Devil. Devil Facial Tumour Disease has infected around 65% of Tasmania's Devil populations since 1996 and has seen numbers plummet in recent years.

the FACTS!

TASMANIA HAS AN AREA of just 68,331 km² and a population of little more than 480,000 people, but more than half a million tourists visit the island each year.

TASMANIA'S COAT OF ARMS shows two Tasmanian Tigers supporting a shield. The motto is *Ubertas et fidelitas*, which means "fruitfulness and faithfulness".

ABEL TASMAN was responsible for both of the island's names. He called the island Anthony Van Diemenslandt (after the then chief of the Dutch East India Company Anthony Van Diemen) in 1642 and its name was later changed from Van Diemen's Land to Tasmania, after the navigator, in a bid to distance the island from its penal past.

HOBART BOASTS Australia's oldest surviving theatre — the Theatre Royal in Campbell Street has been in existence since 1837.

AUSTRALIA'S DEEPEST CAVE and its longest cave are both found in Tasmania. The Anne-A-Kananda Cave is 373 m deep and is located near Mount Anne, while the 17-km-long Exit Cave is found at Ida Bay.

THOUSANDS OF BONE fragments found in Kutikina Cave indicate that Aborigines used the cave for more than 7000 years, probably until rising sea levels in Bass Strait 13,000 years ago led them to abandon the cave.

IN 2003, messages of support from around the globe were sent to the tiny Tasmanian town of Bagdad, which people had confused with the war-torn capital of Iraq.

The Apple Isle, as it is known in Australia, is the smallest State and the only one outside of the mainland. It is a mountainous island resplendent with lakes, pristine wilderness and deep rivers.

HOBART, situated on the Derwent River, is Australia's second-oldest city. It was settled in 1803, largely to capitalise on the sealing and whaling opportunities, but remained a rough, shanty-filled seaman's port until Governor Macquarie implemented public works from 1811. Later, the island became a place of secondary punishment for unrepentant criminals when Port Arthur Prison was constructed in 1830. Of all Australian capitals, Hobart best retains the essence of Australia's colonial past and places such as Battery Point and Salamanca Place hark back to yesteryear. Along with quaint and historic cities and towns such as Launceston, Ross, Bicheno, Richmond, Queenstown and Kingston, Tasmania boasts magnificent wilderness and almost half of the island is preserved in World Heritage Areas, national parks or reserves. World-Heritage-listed wilderness areas include Franklin–Gordon Wild Rivers, Cradle Mountain–Lake St Clair and Walls of Jerusalem National Parks, the Central Plateau Protected Area, Southwest National Park and Hartz Mountains National Park.

Above, top to bottom: Boats moored at historic Victoria Dock; Poppies and tulips in the fields around Table Cape Lighthouse. Opium poppies, used to make morphine, can be legally grown in north-west Tasmania.

GREENS COUNTRY

Tasmania's abundance of protected areas did not come about without the involvement of environmental protesters, who secured the protection of large areas in the 1980s, following the controversial damming of Lake Pedder and the Franklin River "No Dams" protests. Tasmania also saw the establishment of the world's first environmental political party with the formation of the Greens Party in the 1970s. The Greens secure around 10–15% of the vote in climate-conscious Tasmania.

Island Icons

The Tasmanian Devil (*Sarcophilus harrisii,* opposite, far left) is Tasmania's unofficial faunal emblem and the Tasmanian Blue Gum (*Eucalyptus globulus,* left) is its floral emblem.

Above: Hobart is the only Australian capital overlooked by a snow-capped mountain. Mt Wellington may be capped with snow throughout the year and can determine Hobart's daily climate, obscuring the city in low cloud or what the locals call "Bridgewater jerry" fog.

A FEAST FOR THE SENSES

Tasmanian agriculture and organic farming produces some of the freshest, most delectable gourmet produce in Australia. Cool-climate wines, crisp apples, farmed salmon and rich King Island Diary cream and cheese are just some of the foodstuffs exported from this hub of gastronomic activity. The most expensive food item grown in Tasmania is the rare French black truffle. Truffles are grown locally on farms and may fetch as much as $2500/kg at market. Tasmania is also famous for producing two local beers, Cascade (left, Australia's oldest brewery, founded in 1824) in the south and J Boag & Son in the north. Vineyards were established from 1821 (at New Town) and in 1958 Claudio Alcorso established Moorilla Estate on the Derwent River near Hobart. Smaller wineries followed and now a number of vineyards entice visitors to the cellar door. Pipers Brook Vineyard, which dates from 1974, is the oldest winery in northern Tasmania.

DICKENS' INSPIRATION?

Charles Dickens never visited Australia, although his two sons emigrated to the country and many characters in his novels have Australian links. Richmond Gaol in the north of Hobart housed a prisoner named Ikey Solomon, who enlisted young boys to help him with his life of crime. He was believed to be the inspiration for Dickens' character of Fagin in *Oliver Twist.* Solomon's story was also told in Bryce Courtenay's novel *The Potato Factory.*

EAGLEHAWK NECK

During penal days, vicious guard dogs and vigilant guards patrolled the impenetrable Eaglehawk Neck, a natural prison gate near Port Arthur, Tasmania, which deterred convicts from escape. At the neck's narrowest section, eleven dogs were chained, each attached to a pole on which a lantern hung. The fortifications were so extreme that few prisoners even tried to escape, although one, Martin Cash, finally managed to swim past the neck and escape. Another prisoner, William Hunt, dressed himself in a kangaroo skin and attempted to hop to freedom, but gave himself up when the guards spied him and went to shoot the kangaroo to throw in the cooking pot. "Don't shoot!" the startled convict yelled, "It's only me — Billy Hunt!"

CATARACT GORGE

The world's longest single-span chairlift takes visitors over the natural wonder of Cataract Gorge, just a ten-minute walk from Launceston's city centre. Walking tracks around the gorge and reserve, such as the Zig Zag track, include some steep climbs up the cliffs, leading up to the bitingly cold waters of First Basin, Second Basin and Duck Reach and the excellent views from Eagle Eyrie and Cataract lookouts.

Above: Tasmania's ruggedness is typified by Cape Raoul.

the FACTS!

THE PALAWA and Mouheneer Aboriginal people inhabited Tasmania for 35,000 years before Europeans arrived.

THE TREATMENT of Tasmania's Aborigines is among Australia's saddest and most racist history. Tasmanian Aborigines fought fiercely to drive out the settlers, but in 1828 Governor Arthur authorised soldiers to arrest or shoot Aborigines found in areas of European settlement. In 1830, men formed a "Black Line" and walked across Tasmania to flush out and kill Aborigines, but found only two. No pure-blooded Tasmanian Aborigines remained by the early 1900s, although 6500 of their descendants live in Tasmania today. In 1995, the *Tasmanian Aboriginal Lands Act* returned twelve culturally significant sites to Tasmanian Aboriginal people.

PRISONERS HELD in Port Arthur's Model Prison lived in tiny 1.8 by 2.8 m cells that were just 3.3 m high. They were kept in complete silence for 12–18 months of their sentence and were blindfolded when they left their cells so they could not see other prisoners.

IN 1868, a visitor to Scottsdale in Tasmania's north-east noted that the town had "neither police station nor public house, but that people appear to get on harmoniously enough without them". Scottsdale now has pubs and police stations.

ACT
— the nation's capital

the FACTS!

THE ROYAL BLUEBELL (*Wahlenbergia gloriosa*, above) is the ACT's floral emblem.

BEFORE 1901, when Federation turned Australia into a united nation, the six States at the time had separate military forces, politics and law. Federation created an over-arching national framework for law and governance, which took precedence over State law.

OTHER NAMES that were suggested for the capital were Kangermu, Engirscot (combining England, Ireland and Scotland) and the ridiculous Meladneyperbane and Sydmeladperbrisho — combining the names of other State capitals.

THE ACT IS COMPRISED of two land transfers from the State of New South Wales. The first tract of land was set aside in 1915, the smaller area of Jervis Bay was transferred to the Commonwealth for the development of a port. Jervis Bay remains Commonwealth territory.

CANBERRA'S COAT OF ARMS, granted by King George V in 1928, shows a Black Swan to represent the Aboriginal people and a white swan representing European Australians. They bear a shield that shows a three-turreted castle with the Sword of Justice and the parliamentary cross over it. The motto is "For the Queen, the Law and the People".

MORE THAN ONE MILLION blooms enliven Commonwealth Park each September for Floriade.

Following Federation in 1901, people agreed that the site for the new capital had to be outside of the dictates of New South Wales and Victoria. General CS Scrivener recommended the Yass–Canberra area in 1908 and New South Wales transferred 2458 km² to the Commonwealth to facilitate the nation's new capital and seat of governance in the Australian Capital Territory.

CANBERRA IS SITUATED on the slopes of the Molonglo River, which gives it a pleasant bushland setting. In 1911, a competition for the capital's design was won by Chicago architect Walter Burley Griffin, who won £1750 and 3 shillings for his design. He proposed a city nestled amid the three hills of Mt Ainslie, Mt Pleasant and Black Mountain, with a grand parliament house situated in the centre, on Capital Hill, and wide avenues (each representing a State) radiating to outer suburbs. Unfortunately, some of Griffin's concepts were used but other parts of his extravagant design were changed by the departmental board, meaning the final plans were described by some as "a third rate Luna Park". Griffin finally resigned in 1920 and left Canberra in disgust. Vast open parklands and a prominent lake (Lake Burley Griffin), created by the damming of the Molonglo River in

Above: Vibrant balloons take flight over Canberra during the annual Balloon Fiesta.

the 1960s and incorrectly bearing Griffin's middle name as well as his last name, complete the picture of Australia's capital today. Parliament House aside, Canberra is also home to another crucial centre of Australian democracy and judiciary, the High Court of Australia.

Below: Parliament House, one of the biggest buildings in the Southern Hemisphere, is composed of 300,000 cubic metres of concrete, which would be enough to construct 25 Sydney Opera Houses. It was designed by American architect Romaldo Giurgola and finished in 1988, Australia's bicentennial year. The beautiful forecourt mosaic was created by Aboriginal artist Michael Jagamara Nelson.

Above, left to right: Historic Duntroon House, built in 1853, is now the Officer's Mess for Australia's Royal Military College; The Captain Cook Memorial Globe, on the serene shores of Lake Burley Griffin, traces Cook's voyages around the world.

Birds of a Feather

The Gang-gang Cockatoo (*Callocephalon fimbriatum*, below) is the ACT's avian emblem.

FROM PARLIAMENT TO PORTRAITS

Old Parliament House, which was opened by The Duke of York (later George VI) in 1927 and resounded to the strains of Dame Nellie Melba singing the national anthem, was never designed to be a permanent seat of government. Once the grand, modern Parliament House was completed in 1988 another fitting purpose was found for the art-deco "wedding cake" building. It became the National Portrait Gallery but is now the Museum of Australian Democracy.

A TREASURE TROVE OF AUSTRALIANA

Public Servant Percy Deane said of Canberra in 1928, "The best view of Canberra is from the back of a departing train". However, today Australians concede that Canberra is a gracious and beautiful city, especially in the spring and autumn, which does its nation proud. The numerous national attractions and generous surrounding national parks (which cover about half of the Australian Capital Territory), such as Namadji National Park, ensure there are plenty of activities to interest tourists and locals. Galleries and museums showcase the best of Australian history, art and culture and interactive displays at the quirky National Museum of Australia and the National Science and Technology Centre (Questacon) can amuse kids and adults for many hours.

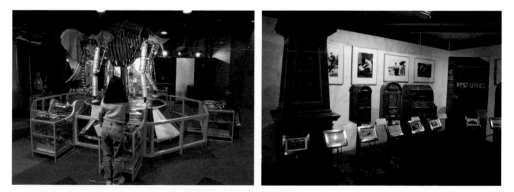

Above, left to right: Displays of science at Questacon, the National Science and Technology Centre; Indigenous and European history are explored at the innovative National Museum.

ART-ENTHUSIASTS CAN IMMERSE themselves in the creative realm at the National Gallery of Australia, which contains masterpieces by recognised Australian artists as well as international talents and the controversial *Blue Poles* by American artist Jackson Pollock. Literature lovers can curl up with a good book at the National Library or take their time examining displays that honour Australian literature and history. The Australian War Memorial also provides a poignant, contemplative setting for those who wish to commemorate Australia's military involvement around the globe. Those seeking to explore the nation's natural treasures can while away the day at the National Zoo and Aquarium at Yarralumla, the National Dinosaur Museum or the magnificent Australian National Botanic Gardens.

the FACTS!

WHILE CANBERRA is believed to mean "meeting place" in a local Aboriginal language, some postulate that it might also mean "women's breasts" (in reference to the hills) or "place of winds".

ORGANISERS THOUGHT over 100,000 people would attend the 1927 opening of parliament and ordered 30,000 pies and sausage rolls — just 6000 people came and ate 10,000 pies; the other 20,000 were buried in a hole on Capital Hill. The overspending made the public service the brunt of many jokes.

FOR MORE THAN A YEAR after Canberra was proclaimed the national capital on 9 May 1927, alcohol was prohibited there. During this time, alcohol sales in the New South Wales' town of Queanbeyan, 11 km from the border, boomed.

CANBERRA'S PUBLIC SERVANTS were given half a day off on a full day's pay to watch a match between two visiting Victorian Rules football teams in 1939. They had to show their entrance tickets with their timesheets to prove they had gone and not just shirked work.

DURING WWII the prudish National Council of Clothing Styles was established in Canberra and dictated what styles women were allowed to wear.

Below: The Deep Space Complex at Tidbinbilla attracts astronomy buffs.

Above: The curious, abstract *Garden of Australian Dreams* outside the National Museum, ACT.

Astounding architecture

From the instantly recognisable Opera House to the glittering, colourful façade of Melbourne's Federation Square, Australia boasts numerous edifices designed to inspire, confound or lend a colonial grace to our cities.

the FACTS!

THE OPERA HOUSE cost around $100 million to build, prompting one wag to joke, "It would have been cheaper if they built it overseas and sailed it across".

NEW SOUTH WALES' PREMIER Jack Lang was supposed to cut the ribbon to open the Sydney Harbour Bridge in 1932, but radical Francis de Groot rode in on a horse and slashed it instead, causing uproar.

PERTH'S 82.5-m-HIGH glass-spired Swan Bell Tower (below), designed by William Hames, houses the only Royal Bells ever to have left England. The bells, which were first cast in the 14th century, once rang in the church of St Martin-in-the-Fields to celebrate the coronation of every British monarch since King George II in 1727. They were a gift to Western Australia, from England, as a part of the bicentennial celebrations in 1998. The tower and its bells combined comprise one of the largest musical instruments in the world.

SONGS OF PRAISE

Many were sceptical of Danish architect Jørn Utzon's design for the Sydney Opera House, construction of which began in 1959, but today it is one of the world's most admired buildings. When Utzon resigned in 1966, irked by Australian bureaucrats who were concerned by the skyrocketing cost in the face of numerous engineering issues, the task was taken over by three Australian architects: Peter Hall, David Littlemore and Lionel Todd. Queen Elizabeth II officially opened the Opera House, which stands on Bennelong Point and is World-Heritage-listed, in 1973. Utzon, did not attend. Although the acoustics inside the building have been criticised, many millions enjoy events at this iconic Opera House each year.

THE STORY OF BRISBANE

Brisbane's Story Bridge is often considered the less-famous sibling of the Sydney Harbour Bridge, but although it shares the same engineer, Dr JC Bradfield, it is an astonishing feat of engineering and is the largest span steel truss bridge designed, fabricated and constructed in Australia. Built during the Great Depression, the highest point of the 1072-m-long (including anchor piers) steel cantilever bridge is 80 m above the Brisbane River.

FEDERATION SQUARE

A mosaic of sandstone, glass and zinc create the unusual colours and geometry of Federation Square, which opened in 2002 and "draws its inspiration from the unique urban characteristics of Melbourne's arcades and lanes".

Above: Huge structural problems were posed by the weight of the Opera House's enormous "sails" and 350,000 man hours were spent on finding a solution. The sails were eventually all produced from a single sphere, rather like the segments of an orange.

Above: The Story Bridge, Brisbane, is named after the former vice-chancellor of the University of Queensland. Four men died during the bridge's construction.

Above: Federation Square, Melbourne, was designed by Lab architecture studio (London) and Bates Smart Architects (Melbourne).

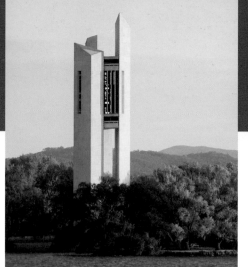

Above: Corrugated iron proved cheap and durable as architectural material during settlement and many heritage-listed pioneer dwellings are made of this classic, outback material. The house above is part of a World-heritage-listed site at Ravenswood, Qld.

NO EXPENSE SPARED

Grandiose Rupertswood Mansion (above) was one of the country's most expensive houses when built by Sir William Clarke in 1874. Clarke's father arrived in Australia in 1829, as a butcher, and bought land at Sunbury for just £1 an acre, accumulating 178,000 acres by the 1890s, making him Victoria's largest landowner. The mansion, which has more than 50 rooms, cost a whopping £25,000 to build and even had its own private railway station. Thomas Chirnside's Werribee Park Mansion was even more expensive, costing £100,000.

A MELODIOUS GIFT

The National Carillon, which sits on Aspen Island in Canberra, ACT, was a gift from the British government to celebrate the 50th anniversary of the nation's capital and was accepted on the public's behalf by Queen Elizabeth II in 1970. It contains 55 bells, the pitch of which ranges through 4.5 octaves. The bells are housed in an angular, three-columned tower of quartz and opal chip designed by WA architects Cameron, Chisholm & Nicol. They are played melodiously by a carillonist and may be heard many kilometres away.

the FACTS!

AUSTRALIA'S NEWEST

Parliament House building, designed by Meldrum Burrows architects and constructed in Darwin, NT, in 1994, divides opinion when it comes to architectural taste. Whatever the "white house's" cynics say, it was designed to combat Darwin's tropical climate and its exterior façade diffuses 80% of direct sunlight entering the building's interior.

SIXTEEN MEN FELL from the Sydney Harbour Bridge while it was under construction. The dead men's colleagues not only had to live with the loss of their friends and the fear of going the same way, they also had to part with half a day's pay for each death — the money being for the dead man's widow.

BRIDGE OF OUR DREAMS

A song written by Len Maurice in 1930 called the famous Sydney Harbour Bridge (below) the "Bridge of Our Dreams Come True" and, once completed in 1932, it certainly captured the Australian imagination. It was also designed by Dr John Bradfield and, with an arch span of 503 m, is one of the most impressive bridges in the world. Work on the bridge began in 1923 and it proved an expensive engineering task, costing £9,577,507 to build, which in today's terms would be about $200 million.

THE REGAL OLD ROYAL

Melbourne's World-Heritage-listed Royal Exhibition Building, which was designed by Joseph Reed and sits in Carlton Gardens, is one of the last surviving 19th-century "world fair" buildings. It was listed on 1 July 2004 and represents "an important interchange of human values, over a span of time". The Duke of York opened Australia's first Federal Parliament in the building on 9 May 1901 and Parliament sat in the building until 1927, when it moved to Parliament House, Canberra, in the newly formed Australian Capital Territory.

LUCKILY, THE TEST designed to measure that the Sydney Harbour Bridge was strong enough for traffic did not fail — if it had, 92 steam engines that had been run onto the bridge would have plummeted into the harbour!

Historic sites
& heritage places

Australia's Indigenous history stretches back aeons, but its European history is just a couple of centuries old. Despite this, Australia's penal past lends some historic places a touch of the macabre and the sites paint a vivid picture of just how difficult colonial life really was.

the FACTS!

FREDERICK MEREDITH, a steward on the HMS *Sirius* scratched out "FM, 1788" on a rock on Garden Island, Sydney Harbour. His un-inventive graffiti remains Australia's oldest surviving record of European settlement.

BRISBANE'S OLDEST BUILDING is the Old Mill on Wickham Terrace (above), which was convict built in 1828. The Commissariat Store in William Street is the only other remaining building from Brisbane's convict era and the first floor was built from 1828–1829. The second floor was added later.

SOUTH AUSTRALIA'S Edicara Fossil Site preserves the world's first record of multicellular animal life on Earth, predating the Cambrian period.

ADELAIDE'S GENERAL POST OFFICE, built from 1867–1872, is one of South Australia's oldest public buildings and is a part of Australia's Commonwealth Heritage.

KIRRIBILLI HOUSE on Sydney Harbour, NSW, was built in the 1850s and has been home to Australian prime ministers from 1957.

Below: Stone ruins of convict barracks near the Nut, Stanley, Tasmania.

UNFORTUNATELY, not a single house from Australia's first 27 years of settlement in New South Wales survives in Sydney today. However, many historic buildings grace nearby Parramatta, including Elizabeth Farm House (1783), the Lancer Barracks (from 1803), Old Government House (1799) and St John's Anglican Church (1803). Cadman's Cottage, which stands at the northern end of George Street in the Rocks is also a historic site and was built in 1813 for Governor Macquarie's coxswain and boat crew.

Above: Rock art galleries around the country record thousands of years of Indigenous spiritual beliefs and Dreaming stories. The most famous galleries are found at Ubirr and Nourlangie (NT), Carnarvon Gorge (Qld), Wollemi NP (NSW), Grampians NP (Vic), Koonalda Cave (SA), the Kimberley (WA) and in Tasmania's south-west caves. Artwork may be drawn to depict spirit ancestors, to request a good hunt, or to work magic.

Above, left to right: Cooks' Cottage, the home of Captain Cook's parents, was shipped to Australia piece by piece and reassembled in Fitzroy Gardens, Vic; La Trobe's Cottage, erected in 1839 is the oldest building in Melbourne. It was later dismantled and moved to Birdwood Avenue. Alterations over the years mean the building is not original.

Below: Port Arthur Historic Site is a grim reminder of Australia's convict past and dates to the 1830s. Thousands of convicts were imprisoned here and millions of visitors each year are chilled by the Guard Tower, prison and other buildings.

NORFOLK ISLAND

Numerous historic sites, including the convict stores (left) are found on Norfolk Island, which was the second colony settled by Europeans in 1788. It was settled twice, with the majority of buildings remaining from the second settlement in 1825. Convict-built Government House, barracks and other buildings at Kingston were built during the Island's time as one of the most hellish penal colonies ever.

SOVEREIGN HILL (VIC)

Sovereign Hill in Ballarat is an outdoor museum that recreates the first decade of life on the Victorian goldfields from 1851. Prospectors and ladies in authentic garb hurry down Main Street to shops that also relive the era. Visitors can even pan for their own gold at the realistic Red Hill Gully Diggings. At night, *Blood on the Southern Cross* re-enacts the Eureka Stockade.

PARONELLA PARK (QLD)

In 1913, José Paronella, from Catalonia, Spain, arrived in Queensland and worked as a sugar-cane cutter then purchased and improved farms until he could afford to build the grand Paronella Park near Cairns. The "castle" was finished in 1935 and housed a theatre, tea gardens, a museum and a hall with a mirrored "disco-ball", as well as gardens and tennis courts. It ran on the State's first hydro-electric power.

THE ROUND HOUSE (WA)

Western Australia's oldest building is the Round House gaol, a twelve-sided building designed by HW Reveley (WA's first engineer). It stands on Arthur Head, Fremantle, and was the first construction in the Swan River colony, completed in 1831. It was used as a police lockup. A tunnel was later built beneath so whalers could access the town from Bathers Beach.

Above, left to right: Blundell's Farm House, built in 1858; Spanish Monks founded the New Norcia monastery in WA in 1847 and named it after the Italian birthplace of St Benedict; A horse-drawn tram adds a touch of yesteryear to historic Victor Harbor, SA.

the FACTS!

THE OLDEST INTACT BUILDING in Victoria is Customs House, which was erected in Geelong in 1838. It was later dismantled and moved to Eastern Park.

WOOLMERS, a private dwelling in Longford, near Launceston, is Tasmania's oldest building and dates from 1818. The 1810 Commissariat Store building is Hobart's oldest building.

ALICE SPRINGS Telegraph Station, in the Northern Territory, dates to 1872. Most of Darwin's buildings were destroyed by cyclone Tracy in 1974; however, the central room of Government House, also dating from 1872, remains.

ST HELENA ISLAND (below), in Moreton Bay, off Brisbane, housed Queensland's most incorrigible convicts from 1867. Around 7% of the original convict buildings remain and visitors can also experience a spooky, night-time "Ghost Tour".

Bushies
— beyond the black stump

There is a certain romance and allure associated with the Australian bush. The continent's impenetrable outback regularly thwarted the efforts of pioneers to tame its waywardness, and remains a vast, lonely place. It is the mysterious, spiritual refuge of resourceful Aborigines and secretive fauna, but it also conjures images of hardy stockmen, brave pioneering women, trudging swaggies, desolation and desperation.

the FACTS!

IN 1883, the MacDonald brothers undertook a gruelling 5600 km trek droving 500 cattle and 50 horses from Goulburn to the Kimberley, where they established the 405,000 ha Fossil Downs station.

RABBITS, a major pest, caused environmental degradation in Australia, but, strangely, Australia's famous national headwear, the Akubra ® (right), is made out of rabbit felt. Five to twelve rabbit pelts are used to make each hat. The hats were first made by English immigrant Benjamin Dunkerley in Tasmania in 1872. The name comes from the Pitjantjatjara word for head covering.

LEATHER BOOTS are a traditional part of outback attire. Tasmanian footwear company Blundstone®, established in 1870, is well known for its iconic boots called Blundstones (shortened to "Blunnies"). The oilskin Driza-Bone® coat, which was based on sailors' wet-weather gear towards the end of the 19th century, is also a must-have item of clothing for stockmen and bushies.

THE "JACKY HOWE", a blue singlet, is a part of the Australian outback uniform. It was named after a gun shearer who tore the sleeves off his shirts and underwear to keep him cool in the woolshed while he shore a record number of sheep.

BOUNDARY RIDERS, drovers and stockmen are the strong and silent icons of the outback. Cattle and sheep stations in the bush are very isolated and can be many thousands of kilometres apart. Often drovers spent months escorting cattle to market. Boundary riders, jackeroos and jillaroos might spend months riding out to check the fences and sleeping rough, with little but horse, swag and billy as creature comforts. Meanwhile, back at the homestead, lonely country wives braved the isolation, knowing they and the children might not receive visitors for many months and, should an accident occur, they had only the flying doctor to rely on.

Above: Skills in droving, breaking in horses, "cutting out" cattle, and wielding a stockwhip are highly regarded in Australia's outback.

CAMPED BY A BILLABONG

"Once a jolly swagman camped by a billabong" — starts what many consider to be Australia's unofficial national anthem, Banjo Paterson's *Waltzing Matilda*. "Humping a bluey" or "waltzing a Matilda" are slang terms for roaming the country carrying only a swag (a canvas bedroll packed with essentials such as billy tea, flour and golden syrup). During the depressions of the 1840s, 1890s and 1930s, many unemployed men set off to seek work as shearers or farmhands, stopping at stations along the way to request food or shelter. It became a custom to give a swaggie at least enough to get him to the next station.

THE LONG PADDOCK

"Long paddocks" provide salvation for outback stations ravaged by drought. These registered stock routes allow graziers to drove herds of stock along the road verges or routes that follow a string of waterholes to keep stock alive in lean times. The introduction of the tiny parasitic Scrub Tick (*Boophilus micropus*) led to the establishment of the famed Canning Stock Route in Western Australia. Tick-infested cattle in the Kimberley were not allowed to be sold at markets in the country's tick-free south in 1898. Cattle barons soon discovered that the ticks required humidity to survive and died if the cattle were driven through the arid dry country. When Alfred Canning followed a route from Halls Creek to the railhead at Wiluna, north-east of Perth, in 1906 and later established 51 wells along the 1753-km route in 1908–1910, the Cattle Kings began to use the path as a stock route to market.

B & S BALLS

Many outback towns are so remote that the chances of finding love are pretty slim, hence available men and women head to a Bachelors and Spinsters Ball, which is often held in a wool shed (with sawdust on the floor) and generally involves a lot of beer and a lot of dancing. B & S Balls became very popular in the 1970s and single young men would drive hundreds of kilometres, with a ute full of beer, to attend.

CLICK GO THE SHEARS

Shearing has provided seasonal work in the country since European settlement. In 1891, the Shearer's Strike was sparked because employers dictated the shearer's working hours and a shearer, once signed on, was unable to leave a property before the shearing was finished without losing his wages. The Australian Labor Party was formed out of the strike and is the oldest surviving Labor party in the world.

the FACTS!

QUEENSLAND'S Bowen Downs station was thought to be the largest sheep station on Earth in 1889 and 364,742 sheep were shorn there that year. Another station, named Burrawang, in NSW, was said to have a shearing board that was so long that "a shearer could get the sack at one end and be re-employed at the other".

ONE OF THE SADDEST situations for country people is to lose the farm through drought or mounting debt. However, "battling on" and starting again from scratch is a typical Aussie trait and rural communities are known to rally around and help each other through hard times.

BUSH POET Adam Lindsay Gordon was such a good horseman that he is said to have jumped his horse over a fence and onto a 1-m-wide plot of land near Blue Lake, Mount Gambier. Behind the 1-m strip, on which the horse and rider balanced precariously, was a steep 60-m drop into the lake. Not only did Gordon persuade his horse to jump across, he then carefully turned the animal around and jumped it back over the old post and rail fence.

THE KELPIE (below) is a farmer's best friend. The breed developed in Ardlethan in New South Wales.

STOCKMAN'S HALL OF FAME

The Australian Stockman's Hall of Fame (above) in Longreach, Queensland, celebrates all things outback. The timber, steel and corrugated iron "shed-like" homage to the bush was conceived by prominent bushies Hugh Sawrey, RM Williams and Dame Mary Durack Miller and opened in April 1988. Its five galleries — Discovery, Pioneers, Outback Properties, Life in the Outback, and Stockworkers — showcase displays such as a traditional drover's campsite, a recreated settler's hut and an old overland telegraph office.

BACK O' BOURKE

The town of Bourke, in the NSW outback, became the unofficial limit of civilisation when the term "back o' Bourke" came into popular use in the late 19th century. Beyond Bourke stretches the vast Australian desert and anything to the "back o' Bourke" was definitely outback. Other terms used to signify the middle of nowhere are "woop woop", "Bullamakanka", "the backblocks" and "beyond the black stump".

Moments that
shook the nation

Above: The Southern Cross flag, a symbol of the Eureka Stockade.

the
FACTS!

IN THE EARLY DAYS of the colony wealthy members of the NSW Corps controlled the sale of rum, which at the time acted like the currency of the colony. Governors Hunter, King and Bligh (formerly Captain of the unlucky *Bounty*) all tried to curb the trade but failed. Eventually, in 1808 the rum barons and the corps treacherously deposed and arrested Governor Bligh (who, embarrassingly, hid under the bed) and took control of the colony in an event that became known as the Rum Rebellion. Order was only restored when Governor Lachlan Macquarie took command in 1811.

ANOTHER UPRISING of the early days — the Eureka Stockade in 1854 — eventually changed the laws of land ownership. Irishman Peter Lalor and other miners in Ballarat, Victoria, were angry at police raids to ensure miners carried expensive licences. They built a fortified stockade and demanded the abolition of licence fees, which they claimed were effectively a type of land tax yet did not entitle them to a vote. Only landholders, which included squatters who paid a small lease fee of less than the mining licences, were able to vote. Soldiers attacked the stockade and put down the revolution but the laws did change and Peter Lalor went on to become a politician.

Even before the moment that truly made the nation, Federation in 1901, some events, such as the Eureka Stockade, played a major role in political and social growth and are embedded in the national psyche. Modern events, both good and bad, also shook and shaped the nation.

THE DISMISSAL

On 11 November 1975, Prime Minister Gough Whitlam was infamously sacked by Governor-General Sir John Kerr — effectively dismissing an elected government that had a majority in the House of Representatives. Two unorthodox appointments to the Senate, in the form of Cleaver Bunton and Albert Field (who had a strong dislike for Whitlam's Labor Government) gave the opposition a stronghold in the Senate, which allowed them to defer consideration of the government's supply and appropriation bills (the budget). This meant that, without a constitutional solution, the government could run out of funds. Remedies, such as calling an election for both parliamentary houses, were dismissed by Whitlam, which led to Kerr handing the PM a prepared dismissal notice on 11 November and appointing Malcolm Fraser as caretaker Prime Minister. An election was called and held on 13 December 1975, returning Malcolm Fraser to the PM's position and prompting some angry voters to call for the abolition of the Crown in Australian governance.

Above: After the dismissal, Whitlam said, "Well may we say 'God save the Queen' because nothing will save the Governor-General".

ATTACKS ON AUSSIE SOIL

On 19 February 1942, Darwin came under fire from 188 Japanese aircraft, which destroyed aircraft, sank eight ships and claimed the lives of at least 243 people, injuring a further 300–400. Although a radio message had warned of a likely attack, the bombs caught Darwin unawares and it was only after they started to fall that the air raid sirens were sounded. By all reports, the bombing was a fiasco and the defence force was in disarray. Darwin was bombed almost 60 times over 21 months. Katherine and Milingimbi (NT); Broome, Derby, Drysdale, Exmouth and Wyndham (WA); and Horn Island, Mossman and Townsville (Qld) were also bombed. However, that was just a forerunner of attacks to come. On 31 May 1942, three Japanese midget submarines penetrated Sydney Harbour and within a week mini subs had shelled both Sydney and Newcastle, torpedoing the naval depot ship *Kuttabul* in Sydney Harbour and killing nineteen people.

Left to right: The Maralinga site was first named X300 but the name Maralinga, which means "thunder fields" in a local Aboriginal language was later used; A banner near the Aboriginal Tent Embassy.

EVENTS THAT DROPPED A BOMBSHELL

On 4 October 1952, Britain exploded its first nuclear bomb on the Monte Bello Islands off Western Australia. Just four years later, further atomic bomb tests were conducted at Maralinga on the edge of the Great Victoria Desert in South Australia and continued until October 1957. Seven bombs were exploded, with the largest being a 25 kiloton bomb. Tests were also carried out on Australian, New Zealand and British servicemen to see how they would withstand a nuclear attack. Traditional Aboriginal owners of the land were also subject to contamination. Despite cleanup efforts, some parts of Maralinga will remain contaminated and radioactive for many thousands of years.

THE CASE THAT SHOCKED AUSTRALIA

When Lindy and Michael Chamberlain (right) began a camping trip to Uluru (then known as Ayer's Rock) in August 1980, they had no idea they were about to become embroiled in judicial proceedings that would shock and scandalise the nation. In a grisly first, their nine-week-old baby daughter Azaria vanished — snatched, her parents insisted, by a prowling Dingo while she slept. However, authorities, media and a public wary of the couple's unorthodox religious beliefs and seeming lack of emotion, were sceptical. After two years of court cases, Lindy was sentenced to life imprisonment for the murder of her child. Michael was convicted for being an accessory to Azaria's murder. Three years later, an inquiry overturned the sentence, releasing the shattered pair. Dingoes are wild animals and recent attacks on children on Fraser Island, Queensland, support the Chamberlain's claims. In 1990, Lindy Chamberlain published her side of the tragic tale in an autobiography *Through My Eyes*. The story was also made into a film starring Meryl Streep.

YIRRKALA PETITION

In 1963, the Yirrkala people of Arnhem Land sent a petition, presented on a piece of bark, to the Menzies government opposing bauxite mining within the Arnhem Land Reserve. The petition failed, but paved the way for the Yirrkala people's 1970 court case against Nabalco and the Commonwealth Government and subsequent native title claims.

Right: In 1982, massive resistance to the Gordon-Franklin Hydro-electric Scheme in Tasmanian's wilderness area saw Australia's first major environmental campaigning. Thousands of protesters blockaded the site and more than 1272 were arrested. The campaign was a success and the Franklin–Gordon Wild Rivers National Park is now part of a World Heritage Area.

the FACTS!

HIS HIGHNESS Prince Alfred — Duke of Edinburgh and the first member of the Royal Family to visit Australia — was shot in the back in Sydney on 12 March 1868 by crazed Irish Fenian sympathiser James O'Farrell. Luckily, the bullet missed the Prince's spine and vital organs as it was (according to surgeons) deflected when it struck the Indian rubber braces the prince wore. James O'Farrell, who had been released from a mental asylum only shortly before the attack, was hanged on 21 April 1868.

ON AUSTRALIA DAY 1972, the Aboriginal Tent Embassy was established on the lawn outside Canberra's Parliament House. The use of the word embassy was significant, indicating that many of Australia's first inhabitants felt like foreigners in their own country, deprived of land and status. The embassies were repeatedly torn down in 1972 and were removed in 1975 before being re-established in 1992. Legal cases such as the Wik and Mabo decisions eventually enabled Aboriginal land rights on Crown Land.

IN 1996, A DEPRAVED GUNMAN seeking to make a name for himself (hence he will remain unnamed here) went on a massacre at the historic site of Port Arthur, killing 35 and wounding many more. His actions disgusted the nation but led to the Howard government implementing strict gun laws and a gun buy-back program aimed at preventing such tragedies in the future.

ON THE OPENING of parliament 2008, the federal government extended a historic apology to Aborigines and Torres Strait Islanders who were removed from their families under assimilation policies in previous decades.

A nation
of warriors

Above: Brave Aborigines, such as Pemulwuy and other warriors, fiercely resisted European takeover and many of the white men expressed admiration for their courage.

the FACTS!

BLOOD WAS FIRST SPILLED on Australian soil for WWI on New Year's Day 1915, when Gool Mahomed and Mullah Abdullah attacked two trains ferrying picnic-goers in Broken Hill, killing four and wounding many more. The men were under the influence of narcotics and had decided to die for their Islamic faith. They flew a Turkish flag from an ice-cream cart and held hundreds of police, soldiers and rifle-toting locals at bay for more than an hour.

ORIGINALLY CALLED Ari Burnu, the less than 1-km stretch of beach where Anzac soldiers struggled ashore at Gallipoli is now called Anzac Cove. The Turks and the Anzacs developed a grudging respect for each other, evidenced by Commander Ataturk's touching 1934 speech, which is engraved on a monument at Anzac Cove and reads in part: *You, the mothers, who sent their sons from far away countries, wipe away your tears/Your sons are now lying in our bosom and are in peace./After having lost their lives on this land they have become our sons as well.*

WHEN THE ANZACS withdrew from Gallipoli, a series of "drip rifles", triggered by a string tied to a dripping bucket of water which slowly rose as the water dripped, were set up to convince the Turks the Anzacs were still there.

AUSTRALIA had the highest casualty rate, per population, of any Allied force in WWI.

War, whether between Indigenous warriors and European settlers or in the theatres of Europe or South-East Asia in the 1900s, has helped shape the nation's character and looms large in the collective Australian consciousness. Commemorating the sacrifices of veterans and revering their determination, mateship, grit and humour in adversity remains an important part of Australian culture.

Above: Soldiers in the trenches go "Over the top" in Ypres, Belgium, during World War I.

WORLD WAR I (1914–1918) and World War II (1939–1945) saw the greatest loss of Australian life overseas, but they were not the first wars Australia had been involved in. Troops had previously been sent to Sudan in 1885 and to the Boer War in 1899. Early in 1901, a naval contingent was also sent to China after the Boxer Rebellion. However, Australia's contribution to WWI, as the Allies' only all-volunteer force, was remarkable and young soldiers of the newly federated nation proved themselves among the bravest and most loyal in the world. World War II was to rock the young nation's sense of security when attacks on Australian soil were made for the first time and the loyalty of Allies was tested in the battle of the Pacific. Just five years after WWII finished, Australia honoured the UN's call for troops to intervene in the Korean War (1950–1953) and later became embroiled in the controversial Vietnam War (1962–1975). Australian forces have also recently served or played a peacekeeping role in the Gulf War, Dili, Afghanistan and Iraq.

THE LIGHT HORSE BRIGADE

During WWI, on 31 October 1917, Australians in the 4th (Victorian) and 12th (NSW) Light Horse Regiments made an audacious raid on the Palestinian town of Beersheeba. The Turkish stronghold had wells and the Australian troops desperately needed water for their horses. The commander of the Light Horse Brigade, Lieutenant-General Sir Henry Chauvel, commanded a full frontal assault over 3 km of open ground. The men formed three lines behind a rise about 6.5 km away from the town and, by the time the first line reached 2 km away, the horses were coming on at a gallop. The Turks fired rifles, machine guns and even aircraft fire at the rapidly approaching Australians, who quickly descended upon them and engaged the Turks in hand-to-hand combat. The charge of the Light Horse Brigade succeeded only by sheer audacity. However, the Light Horse suffered only light casualties, with 31 dead and 36 injured, and took the town of Beersheeba.

Right: Models at the Australian War Memorial recreate the charge of the Light Horse Brigade.

Above, left to right: Military intelligence was crucial in the Korean and Vietnam wars, where the enemy was often hidden; A diorama display of diggers scaling the parapets at Gallipoli in WWI; Steve Parish with some of today's young soldiers in Port Douglas.

SOME OF THE BLOODIEST fighting of WWI was in the muddy trenches of France and Belgium where more than 5000 men of the Australian Fifth Division were slaughtered in just half an hour in July 1916. However, the battle that highlighted the strength of the Australian character was the catastrophic defeat of the Gallipoli campaign, in which 8709 Australians and 2701 New Zealand Anzacs lost their lives. A military blunder saw the men land on a beach facing steep, heavily fortified cliffs, but tales of stoicism, heroism and friendship in the face of defeat resonate with Australians to this day.

DURING WWII, more than 15,000 soldiers were captured by the Japanese in the fall of Singapore and the word Changi became synonymous with the horrors of being a prisoner of war. Many of the men were forced to work on the Burma Railway, where around 2800 Australians perished, mostly of malnutrition, exhaustion, malaria and tropical diseases. Closer to home, poorly trained conscript "chocolate soldiers" braved the horrors of the Kokoda Track in New Guinea, where they fought the Japanese in dense jungle, carrying their wounded mates up treacherously steep, muddy trails with the help of locals.

WE WERE THE RATS

Four Australian infantry brigades fought in North Africa in WWII and held off attacks by the Germans and Italians in Tobruk, Libya, in December 1941. The starving Allies were disparagingly called the "Rats of Tobruk" by the Axis troops because they scavenged for food. The troops later proudly took up the name for themselves. Jack Lawson Glassop later wrote the famous novel *We Were the Rats* about the siege.

FOR VALOUR

Ninety-seven Australians have received the Victoria Cross, Australia's highest military honour which is inscribed with the words "For Valour". Three medallists from WWI even re-enlisted in WWII, including the famous Wally Brown, who enlisted at the age of 54 (the maximum age was 40). Four Victoria Crosses were awarded to Australian soldiers in Vietnam.

AN UN-WINNABLE WAR?

Many Australians were opposed to troops being sent to Vietnam to support the USA and South Vietnam against the North Vietnamese and insurgent Viet Cong in 1964. And, later, conscription further inflamed the issue. The guerilla warfare of the enemy limited the effectiveness of conventional weapons and the feeling was that Australians had become bogged down in a war they couldn't win. While Australian politicians argued about whether to bring troops home, by May 1970 around 200,000 anti-Vietnam protesters marched in Australia's capital cities. When troops began to be withdrawn in 1970 and conscription was abolished by the Whitlam government in 1972, Australians were urged to forget that the nation had ever been involved in the "war we should not have been in". Of course, it was impossible for those who had fought in Vietnam to forget and many

Veterans of battles such as Long Tan and Bien Hoa were denied compensation or treated with disdain by a war-weary public. Today, Australians honour the commitment and sacrifice of the some 40,200 Australians who served in Vietnam knowing that the words "Lest we forget" apply to all sacrifices made by all Australian troops.

Right: Soldiers at Nui Dat, Vietnam, enjoy a rare peaceful BBQ on "thongs day".

the FACTS!

CONSCRIPTION WAS TWICE rejected by referendums during WWI and although conscripts were called up during WWII, they were assigned only home duties or to fight in the Pacific campaign to save Australia from invasion. The introduction of conscription (the "Death Lottery") in 1964 divided the nation.

INDIGENOUS Papua New Guineans were known as "Fuzzy-wuzzy Angels" for helping carry wounded Australian troops through the dense jungles to safety in WWII.

LEN WATERS became Australia's only Aboriginal fighter pilot in the RAAF in World War II and flew an American Kittyhawk P-40 M fighter plane, aptly named *Black Magic,* in New Guinea and Borneo. The plane's name was pure coincidence — it got its name because its previous owner was named John Blackmore.

DIGGER WAS A TERM first used in the Victorian goldfields and later in the trenches of WWI when one man said, "we are not soldiers, we are diggers" because the men spent so much time digging trenches. In Vietnam, dogs sniffed out landmines, ammunitions dumps and Viet Cong tunnels and became known as "four-legged diggers".

THE DICKIN MEDAL is a bronze medallion engraved with "For Gallantry, We Also Serve" and is for animals. From 1943–1949, pigeons received 32 Dickin Medals (two Australian pigeons among them), dogs got eighteen, three went to horses and one went to a cat named Simon aboard the HMS *Amethyst.*

Above: Sir Edward Dunlop was a surgeon and saviour during WWII.

Heroes, larrikins
& legends

The men and women of Australian legend are a mixed bunch; some were selfless, courageous war heroes, others were merely good samaritans who recognised the need to help others. Yet others were larrikins and bushrangers, who laughed in the face of authority and did as they pleased. All of them combine to create a rich tapestry of folklore and human history.

AUSTRALIA IS A LAND THAT HAS ALWAYS been steeped in legend. Indigenous Dreaming stories record the legends of an ancient, mystical people, and the Europeans who settled these shores from 1788 added further tales of courage to the litany of legend.

BUCKLEY'S AND NONE

Legendary William Buckley, the "Wild White Man", was an escaped convict who lived with Aborigines for more than three decades until Surveyor John Wedge came across the heavily tattooed, possum-skin-clad man at Indented Head near Geelong, Victoria, in 1835. He had even forgotten how to speak English. Buckley's amazing life coined the colloquial phrase "Buckley's" or "Buckley's and none" to refer to a very slim chance of something happening in a person's favour.

the FACTS!

ONE OF THE NATION'S most revered war heroes is "Weary" Dunlop, who joined the Australian military corps as a doctor and fought in World War II. In true, obscure Aussie nickname tradition, he was not called weary because he was tired from relentlessly saving men's lives (which he did) but because an advertising slogan for Dunlop's tyres went "they wear well", hence he became "weary". Dunlop was captured in 1942 in Java and sent to the Burma Railway, where he set up a hospital of sorts and tended to 5600 Australian soldiers. Sir Edward "Weary" Dunlop received a State funeral in 1993.

DAWN FRASER was once told she would never swim for Australia because of her working-class origins, which spurred on her swimming career. Fraser won the same event at three Olympic Games in a row and maintained her world record in the 100 m freestyle for fifteen years. She set 39 world records and won more Olympic medals than any Australian at the time. Unfortunately, her larrikin nature put an end to her career when she allegedly "souvenired" a flag from the Japanese Emperor's palace during the 1964 Tokyo Olympics and was banned for ten years.

SIXTEEN-YEAR-OLD HEROINE
Grace Bussell coaxed her horse into plunging seas to rescue survivors of the shipwrecked *Georgette* in 1876. This prompted a young surveyor to read her story in the paper, declare that this was the woman he would marry, and ride 300 km to make her his bride! Their two sons became decorated WWI heroes.

BREAKER MORANT

Harry Morant first made a name for himself as a poet and a horseman, arising in his nickname "Breaker". In 1899, he enlisted in the South Australian Mounted Rifles and was sent to South Africa in 1900, where he was promoted to sergeant before being discharged. He later returned to South Africa and enlisted with the Bushveldt Carbineers, which comprised British, Boers and colonials. When Morant's commander, Captain Frederick Hunt, was killed in a fight with Boers — Morant, then second in charge, took command and a series of bloody reprisals on the Carbineers' Boer prisoners followed. Their own men protested and Morant and Handcock were committed for trial and found guilty of the deaths of nine Boer prisoners. They swore they were following earlier orders received by British Captain Hunt, because the British did not "want prisoners to flood the concentration camps", but they were executed by a firing squad on 27 February 1902. Many Australians believed the men had been made scapegoats for British atrocities in South Africa. Above all, it was probably Morant's last words that made him a folk hero. He is believed to have said to his 18-men firing squad, "Shoot straight, you b*stards! Don't make a mess of it".

Above, right: Harry "Breaker" Morant become an Australian folk hero, but in fact he was born in Bridgewater England on 9 December 1864 and arrived in Australia as an immigrant in 1883.

Left to right: Dad and Dave; Men dressed as the Kelly Gang at an Australia Day parade. The gang's acts, such as burning record books and deeds when they robbed banks, were seen as heroic by poor farmers who were heavily in debt to the banks.

COURAGEOUS OR KILLERS?

The Kelly Gang — the most famous bushrangers in Australian history — terrorised locals and travellers across southern New South Wales and north-east Victoria for two years until they were outnumbered by police in the small town of Glenrowan in June 1880. The gang believed that the Kelly family had been unfairly persecuted by the police when Ned and Dan Kelly's mother was arrested and gaoled for shooting at a constable, and Ned, who had been absent at the time, was implicated. The gang robbed banks in Euroa and Jerilderie and shot dead three police officers. Ned's famous 7500-word Jerilderie Letter, which painted him as a crusader against a corrupt police force, was not published at the time because it was deemed "clearly written for the purpose of exciting public sympathy for the murderers". In the letter, Ned wrote, "I would like to know what business an honest man would have in the Police as it is an old saying 'It takes a rogue to catch a rogue'". Ned Kelly survived the Glenrowan shoot out, but his younger brother Dan and friends Steve Hart and Joe Byrne were killed. Ned was found guilty of murder and hanged on 11 November 1880. His famous last words were, "Such is life".

SIMPSON & HIS DONKEY

John Simpson Kirkpatrick and his donkey create one of the more enduring symbols of Australian mateship in wartime. Simpson enlisted in the 3rd Field Ambulance Unit in 1914 and was among the first to land in Gallipoli on 25 April 1915. Using donkeys, he transported wounded soldiers to the field ambulance dressing stations and became an encouraging sight as he entered and emerged unscathed from the heavily shelled Shrapnel Gully up to fifteen times a day. Simpson was killed on 19 May by a shell burst, but his donkey ferried its last passenger to safety before returning to where its master's body lay.

Left: A commemorative sculpture of Simpson and his donkey, named Duffy, stands outside the Australian War Memorial.

LITERARY LARRIKINS

In the early 1940s, James McAuley and Hal Stewart, incensed by the "gradual decay of meaning and craftsmanship in poetry" wrote 16 nonsensical poems in one afternoon and sent them to the *Angry Penguins* literary magazine under the fake name Ern Malley. The poems were a mix of quotes, parts of Shakespeare's plays and words randomly chosen from a dictionary. The editor took the bait, calling Ern Malley a "poet of tremendous power". Strangely, the editor was then prosecuted for publishing indecent poetry when one Detective Vogelsang objected to the poem *Night Piece*, which began with "*The intemperate torch grazed/ With fire the umbrel of the dark*". Vogelsang, the sole Crown witness, said, "Apparently, someone is shining a torch in the dark. To my mind they were going there for some disapproved motive. I have found that people who go into parks at night go there for immoral purposes". The editor was found guilty of indecency and fined £10 plus court costs. Ironically, other writers, while questioning the creators' motives, agreed that Ern Malley was a fine poet.

Myths
& mysteries

the FACTS!

Vanishing politicians, haunted gaols and other mysterious goings on captivate and confound.

Above: Phar Lap, whose name means "lightning" in Siamese, winning the 1930 Melbourne Cup.

ACCORDING TO OFFICIAL REPORTS, the last Tasmanian Tiger died in Hobart in 1936, but that does not quell rumours that the tiger still lives. Around 4000 sightings have been reported since, although a convincing photo has never surfaced. Rewards, including a $100,000 offer by American Ted Turner in 1983 and *The Bulletin's* $1.25 million reward in 2005, have failed to turn up any trace. Entrepreneur Peter Wright also spent $250,000 on a search for the Thylacine in 1985. Such attempts indicate the animal is almost certainly extinct. However, Professor Michael Archer and his team began a new mission to try to clone DNA from a Tasmanian Tiger in 1999 and advances in genetic sequencing technology might mean that the Tassie Tiger (top) may once again prowl these shores.

IN JANUARY 1998, Americans Tom and Eileen Lonergan went missing off St Crispins Reef on the Great Barrier Reef after being accidentally left behind by a dive boat. But was it an accident? The boat operators' reports of a miscount indicate it was, but the Lonergans' journals, found in their hotel room, hinted at personal problems and some people believe they may have faked their deaths. Their bank accounts and insurance policies remain untouched.

SEVERAL PLANES mysteriously disappeared over Bass Strait during the 1930s and were reported in the media at the time. Explanations for what happened to these aircraft have never been given.

CONTROVERSIAL hooded figures in Kimberley rock art found in 1838 are called *Wandjinas* (the spirit in the cloud) by Aborigines. Some believe they depict extraterrestrial life, but anthropologists find them consistent with local Aboriginal mythology.

NEW ZEALAND-BORN, 17.1-hands high Phar Lap, or "Big Red" is Australia's most famous racehorse and his death remains an enduring conspiracy theory. He won his first race in April 1929 and went on to win the Melbourne Cup in 1930. He was such a favourite to win that two men attempted a drive-by shooting to kill the horse, who was saved by the intervention of his strapper, Tommy Woodcock. Phar Lap won five major races in 14 days at the 1930 Spring Racing carnival, prompting jockey Jimmy Pike to say, "They can breed 'em with wings on and get Kingsford Smith to ride em, and I doubt whether they'll beat him". In 1931, special handicapping meant Phar Lap was to carry an unheard of 68 kg of extra weight, not surprisingly, he did not win and was taken to America to compete in the Agua Caliente Handicap — the richest horse race in the world at the time. He won, but it was to be his last victory. Sixteen days later, Phar Lap's devoted strapper awoke to find the gelding distressed and running a temperature. Soon after midday the horse mysteriously collapsed and died, amid rumours he had been poisoned. Two autopsies were conducted but proved inconclusive and colic was given as a possible cause of death. Phar Lap's skeleton was sent to New Zealand, his hide to Melbourne (where it was painstaking recreated) and his exceptionally large heart to Canberra, although some claim the huge heart was actually the heart of a draught horse. In 2006, the Australian Synchotron Research Program wrote a report stating, "arsenic in the horse's hair structure was consistent with a large, single dose of arsenic".

MYSTERIOUS MIN MIN LIGHTS

Since 1918, hundreds of travellers in the outback near Winton and Boulia in north-west Queensland have reported a light (sometimes two or more) eerily appearing in the sky. Legend has it a stockman was first to see the light, hovering over a grave in the small town of Min Min. He galloped to the next station but the luminescent object followed. The Min Min Light has been reported by groups, couples, solo stockman, miners, drivers and bushwalkers. Some people believed the lights were UFOs, others that they were peaceful spirits; however, recent studies by Professor Jack Pettigrew at the University of Queensland provide a natural explanation — the lights are caused by light refraction. The effect is known as Fata Morgana and occurs when a dense layer of cold air is trapped close to the ground beneath a layer of warm air. Light near the ground is then refracted on a curved path and cannot disperse. Effectively, the light is carried hundreds of kilometres away and can be seen by an observer who is not in a line of direct vision to the original source. Professor Pettigrew replicated the light in a natural setting (from car headlights in a low watercourse out of view of six observers — the light appeared to float on the horizon above the watercourse) and in the laboratory. The flat channel country around Boulia provides the perfect setting for this effect to occur. Less romantic than the legend of the Min Min Light perhaps, but equally as remarkable.

The Mythical Bunyip

The bunyip is a mythological water-dwelling monster that the Aborigines believed made loud noises, lived in billabongs and devoured women and children.

the FACTS!

A MR CALVERT reported sighting a bunyip in south-western NSW in November 1868. He tried to trample it with his horse and said that if it wasn't a bunyip it was probably a large otter. He also said, "It is all nonsense about its being a savage sort of brute, as it never left a mark on my horse and it was nearly all the time under his feet".

WHEN THE *HIGH AIM 6* was found steaming towards the Western Australian coast on 4 January 2003, officials were amazed to discover tonnes of rotting fish on board but not a single member of the vessel's crew. The fishing vessel had been reported missing in the Pacific, close to the Marshall Islands, and an empty life raft was found by the US coastguard. Two years' worth of investigations failed to unearth what happened to the captain, engineer and ten Indonesian crew of the ghost ship, which was eventually dismantled.

ONE OF THE MOST ENDURING mysteries in the history of Australian exploration is the disappearance of Ludwig Leichhardt and his men in 1848. They were last seen at Muckadilla Creek, Qld, and despite Augustus Gregory finding many trees engraved with an L, the men's bodies have never been found.

DO THE SOULS of the 136 prisoners hanged at Old Melbourne Gaol (including the infamous Ned Kelly) haunt the dim corridors at night? Who really knows for sure? Paranormal researcher Darren Done has used microphones and surveillance cameras to search the historic 1840-built gaol and has witnessed at least three unexplained events. Events include mysterious orbs of light, a cry for help (apparently heard on the day a former inmate had killed herself) and, exactly one year later, an eerie Irish voice was taped saying "get out".

FACT OR FICTION?

On St Valentine's Day 1900, three schoolgirls and their teacher vanish amid the mysterious monoliths of Hanging Rock — so goes Joan Lindsay's 1967 novel *Picnic at Hanging Rock*, which haunts visitors to the rock to this day. The book is almost certainly fictional, but Lindsay's obscure note — "Whether *Picnic at Hanging Rock* is fact or fiction, my readers must decide for themselves. As the fateful picnic took place in the year 1900, and all the characters who appear in this book are long since dead, it hardly seems important" — only adds to the enigma. Many people report an uncannily eerie feeling at the rock, but no police or media reports of schoolgirls disappearing there have ever been found and

the date Lindsay gives as a Saturday was actually a Wednesday in 1900. The reserve's ranger has received parcels in the mail from superstitious folk as far away as Ireland, returning fragments of stolen rock, explaining that the stone had brought them nothing but trouble. In 2002, a young boy slipped and fell to his death on Hanging Rock and a plaque reminds visitors, who ascend the stairs beneath the hulking, suspended slab, of the true dangers to be found there.

Left: Two girls exploring Hanging Rock, a geological phenomenon near Melbourne, Victoria.

WHAT HAPPENED TO HAROLD HOLT?

Only the prime minister of a laidback country like Australia could slip into the surf one day without any security protection and disappear without a trace. That is what happened on 17 December 1967, when Prime Minister Harold Holt vanished off Cheviot Beach on the Mornington Peninsula, Victoria. Conspiracy theories abounded — was he attacked by a shark? Did he drown after suffering a heart attack? Or was he kidnapped and assassinated? The most unlikely theory put forward was that he was abducted by CIA scuba divers because he was a spy for the Chinese!

A friend, Alan Stewart, allegedly saw Mr Holt enter the water at 11.15 am and said he appeared to drift further and further from the shore until he eventually disappeared. The Army, Navy, Air Force and police all conducted extensive searches but failed to recover Mr Holt's body. The surf was extremely rough that day, with 1.8 m waves crashing on the beach, so the real mystery remains as to why Mr Holt entered the treacherous water in the first place, if, indeed, he actually did!

Right: Harold Holt, shown here with his daughters-in-law, was a passionate skin diver.

Australian
artists & authors

the
FACTS!

ONE OF NORMAN LINDSAY'S
(above) nude paintings *The Crucified Venus* was considered too obscene to be exhibited, but Julian Ashton, founder of the famous art school and gallery, refused to remove it and reached a ludicrous compromise, hanging it to face the wall.

WHEN THE WEALTHY FOUNDER
of *The Bulletin*, JF Archibald, died in 1919, he set aside money in his will as a prize for outstanding Australian portraiture. The Archibald Prize, established in 1921, is today one of Australia's most highly revered and often-controversial artistic awards.

PORTRAIT PAINTER William Dobell won the Archibald Prize in 1943 with the controversial Joshua Smith portrait. Critics argued that the portrait was actually a caricature and Dobell became disenchanted with the Australian art scene.

TOM ROBERTS, along with Arthur Streeton and Charles Condor, formed the famous Heidelberg School of artists renowned for their impressionist paintings.

SO-CALLED ANGRY DECADE
artists such as Sidney Nolan and Albert Tucker challenged the convention and complacency of Australian art and developed an abstract, contemporary style.

ACCLAIMED PORTRAITIST Tom Roberts' famous *Bailed Up* (below) depicts an incident from the 1860s on the old Armidale to Inverell Road at Inverell, NSW.

From the Heidelberg School of impressionists to Pro Hart and Sidney Nolan, Australia has produced a slew of world-renowed artists whose works command gallery space around the globe.

THE FIRST ART produced in Australia recorded the country's unique natural history, with artists such as Sydney Parkinson, John Lewin and Georgiana McCrae painstakingly recreating plant and animal life. The first professional artist was probably Conrad Martens in 1835, whose work was largely confined to landscapes. Later, in the 1880s, the formation of the Heidelberg School furthered Australian landscape painting and it was not until after WWI that modernist, abstract and portraiture artworks began to be widely created. In the 1970s, Aboriginal artwork came to the fore, followed in the 1980s by the vivid works of Ken Done and Pro Hart. Today's artists incorporate a variety of media and styles.

Left: Brett Whiteley produced uninhibited pieces of artistic expression and tried to portray "life force and its insoluble conflicts". This sculpture, *Almost Once*, stands outside the Art Gallery of New South Wales.

Below, right: Sir Arthur Streeton was a talented landscape artist and official World War I artist. Many of his works, including this watercolour of the ruins of the Church of St Jean, Peronne, France, hang at the Australian War Memorial.

ALBERT NAMATJIRA

Arrernte man Albert Namatjira (below left) was one of the most celebrated artists of the 1950s and 60s, expertly capturing the beauty and desolation of Central Australia. Namatjira began his career carving wooden plaques out of Mulga wood, but was soon earning more than £1000 for an exhibition under the guidance of watercolour artist Rex Bartabee. The Aboriginal tradition of sharing among relatives meant that his wealth was distributed among as many as 500 people and, although he was Aboriginal and denied a vote, he still had to pay income tax. When he applied to buy a house in Alice Springs in 1951, he was denied permission because Aborigines were not allowed in town after dark. However, hypocritically, three years later, in 1954, he was taken to Sydney, dressed in a white suit, to meet the Queen of England. Namatjira was sent to gaol for six months in 1958 for supplying his relatives with alcohol and died shortly afterwards.

Right: Blinky Bill, the Quaint Little Australian, was first developed by author and artist Dorothy Wall in 1933 and quickly became a children's classic.

BATTLE OF THE BUSH BALLADEERS

Andrew Barton "Banjo" Paterson (above left) and Henry Lawson (above centre) are Australia's two most famous bush poets and their visions of life in the bush and the city in the 1880s are lasting records of Australia in the late 19th century. Paterson was born near Orange, New South Wales, in 1864 and, despite the humble origins of many of his ballads, actually trained as a lawyer and journalist and was a war correspondent in the Boer War and WWI. His best known poems are *Clancy of the Overflow*, *Waltzing Matilda* and *The Man from Snowy River*. Lawson was born in Grenfell in 1867 and was the son of feminist writer Louisa Lawson. He was an accomplished short story writer as well as a poet, publishing famous collections *While the Billy Boils* and *In the Days When the World was Wide*, as well as classic poems such as *Andy's Gone with Cattle*. The two poets engaged in poetic rivalry throughout 1892, publishing competing witty poems, such as *Up the Country* (Lawson) and *In Defence of the Bush* (Paterson) in *The Bulletin*, but, in fact, they were friends and Banjo Paterson used his solicitor skills to check Lawson's publishing contracts. In 1939, Paterson told the *Sydney Morning Herald* that Lawson had said of their rivalry, "We ought to be able to get in three or four sets of verses before they stop us". Paterson added, "So we slam-banged away at each other for weeks and weeks; not until they stopped us, but until we ran out of material".

MAY GIBBS' BABIES

May Gibbs was born in January 1877 in Kent, England, and went on to become one of Australia's most successful children's authors and illustrators. She published *Gumnut Babies* in 1916, followed by the hugely successful *Snugglepot & Cuddlepie* in 1918, *Little Blossom* in 1920 and *Little Obelia* in 1921. Her interpretation of Australian flora as cherubic children terrorised by the scraggly "Big Bad Banksia Men" delighted generations of Australian children and continue to do so.

We're still above Water!

AWARD-WINNING AUTHORS

Australia's only Nobel Prize winner for Literature to date is Patrick White (left), who was awarded the honour in 1973. White's novels explored Australia's convict era, settlement and social existence, with his most famous, *The Tree of Man*, published in 1955. Other acclaimed Australian novelists include Ethel Turner (*Seven Little Australians*), Xavier Herbert (*Capricornia, Poor Fellow My Country*), David Malouf (*Johnno*), Tim Winton (*Cloudstreet*), Katherine Susanna Pritchard (*Coonardoo*),Thomas Keneally (*Schindler's Ark*), Peter Carey (*Oscar and Lucinda*), Thea Astley (*The Acolyte*), Ruth Park (*The Harp in the South, Playing Beattie Bow*), Colleen McCullough (*The Thorn Birds*) and Colin Thiele (*Storm Boy*).

the FACTS!

POET HENRY KENDALL (top right) published *Songs from the Mountain* in 1880 and is regarded as one of Australia's finest lyrical poets. He led a troubled life and had previously been committed to the Gladesville Hospital for the insane. Kendall died in 1882.

THE FIRST NOVEL published in Australia was ex-convict Henry Savery's autobiographical *Quintus Servington*, which was published in Hobart in 1830. Other popular convict-themed books were John Lang's *Botany Bay* (1859) and Marcus Clarke's *For the Term of His Natural Life*, published in 1874.

ROLF BOLDREWOOD (aka Thomas Browne), a police magistrate, penned the popular *Robbery Under Arms*, glorifying Australian bushrangers, and published it as a three volume novel in 1889.

CJ DENNIS became one of Australia's best-loved poets when he published *The Songs of the Sentimental Bloke* in 1915.

KENNETH SLESSOR, Judith Wright, Kath Walker (Oodgeroo Noonuccal), Bruce Dawe, David Malouf and Les Murray are other famous Australian poets.

MANY WOMEN authors published under male pen names because it was not considered "proper" for ladies to write. They included Stella Maria Franklin (Miles Franklin, below) and Ethel Richardson (Henry Handel Richardson).

Famous
Australians

the
FACTS!

WHEN COMEDIAN Barry Humphries created the suburban housewife Edna Everage (above, a pun on the word average) in 1955, he had no idea she would go on to became a household name (and a Dame no less) or that her introduction "Hello Possums" and her love of gladiolis would become so recognisable worldwide.

FLAMBOYANT ENTERTAINER and Academy Award-winner Peter Allen, who was born in Tenterfield, NSW, is best known for his emotive song "I Still Call Australia Home".

DAME NELLIE MELBA and Dame Joan Sutherland are world-renowned Australian opera singers. Dame Melba sang the national anthem at the 1927 opening of Parliament House in Canberra.

AT JUST THIRTY YEARS of age, Australian-born actor George Lazenby starred as 007 in the 1969 bond movie *On Her Majesty's Secret Service*, making him the youngest Bond and the only Australian Bond.

HANDSOME, HEDONISTIC movie star Errol Flynn (below) was born in Hobart, Tasmania, in 1909. He became famous playing Fletcher Christian in *In the Wake of the Bounty* in 1932 and shot to Hollywood stardom, making 60 films from 1936–1942.

For a sparsely populated country that is so far away from the sophistication of America and Europe, Australia has still managed to make its mark on the world stage. Many Australians are world-famous, be it as politicians, philanthropists, fashionistas, movie stars or media magnates.

THE WORLD'S SCREENS and stages have been graced by many famous Australian movie stars and actors, including Chips Rafferty, Bud Tingwell, Judy Davis, Nicole Kidman, Russell Crowe, Guy Pearce, Hugh Jackman, Hugo Weaving, Mel Gibson, Sam Neill, Cate Blanchett, the late Heath Ledger, Toni Collette, Rachel Griffiths and Geoffrey Rush, to name a few! Cinema-goers have also laughed along with Australian movies such as *Crocodile Dundee*, *Muriel's Wedding*, *Priscilla Queen of the Desert* and *The Castle*, all of which parody Australian culture. More serious films include *Rabbit Proof Fence*, *Ten Canoes*, *Lantana, Shine* and the musical *Moulin Rouge*. Theatre in Australia began in the 1790s but came to true prominence when George Coppin arrived in 1843 and began bringing troupes of performers to entertain the crowds.

Above: Two home-grown talents, Nicole Kidman and Hugh Jackman, on the film set of Baz Luhrmann's epic *Australia* in May 2007.

MEMORABLE AUSTRALIAN PMS

Edmund Barton (1901–03) The first PM
Andrew Fisher (1908–15) Three times PM
William Hughes (1915–23) WWI PM nicknamed the "Little Digger". He represented four different political parties over his 58-year parliamentary career.
Earle Page A caretaker PM who held the position for just 25 days in April 1939.
Robert Menzies (1939–41,1949–1966) Australia's longest-serving PM was twice elected. Declared Australia's involvement in WWII.
John Curtin (1941–45) Newspaper editor turned PM during WWII's Pacific campaign. He never lived to see peace, dying just a month before the war ended.
Ben Chifley (1945–49) A humble post-war PM who had been a train driver before becoming a politician.
Harold Holt (1966–67) The only PM to vanish while in office.
John Gorton (1968–71) The only PM to have voted himself out of office!
Gough Whitlam (1972–75) The only PM to be "sacked" by the governor-general.
Malcom Fraser (1975–83) Asked to take over following the dismissal.
Bob Hawke (1983–91) Ousted from office by a leadership challenge within his party.
Paul Keating (1991–96) Gave us "the recession we had to have".
John Howard (1996–2007) Australia's second-longest serving PM.
Julia Gillard (2010–2013) Australia's first female PM (see below).
Kevin Rudd (2007–2010, 2013–) Resigned in 2010 after being challenged by his deputy, Julia Gillard. Rudd became PM for a second time in 2013 after defeating Gillard in a party leadership ballot.

Left to right: Charles Kingsford Smith; On 25 November 1981, Pat O'Shane became simultaneously the first woman and the first Aborigine to head a government department; Sir Douglas Nicholls became the first Aborigine to be knighted, in 1972. Four years later he became the 28th Governor of South Australia.

FLYING MACHINES

Two world-famous aviators hailed from Queensland. Bert Hinkler was born in Bundaberg and become renowned for making the longest solo flight the world had seen in 1928 — from England to Australia in just fifteen days, two hours and 45 minutes. He was a very private man who became known as the "Lone Eagle". When Hinkler died in an aeroplane crash in Italy in 1933, dictator Benito Mussolini organised his funeral. Sir Charles Kingsford Smith, after whom Sydney Airport (or Kingsford Smith International Airport) is named, was Brisbane-born and pioneered air routes from Australia around the world, being the first to fly across the Pacific to America (along with his friend and fellow aviator Charles Ulm). *The Southern Cross*, his most famous plane, can be seen at Brisbane Airport.

FROM A LAND DOWN UNDER

Since Rock and Roll was born, the world has been rocked by Australian music that went international. One of the first performers to come to the world's attention was "the wild one" Johnny O'Keefe and his success was followed by that of Little Pattie, the Easybeats, the Skyhooks, Col Joye, The Seekers, The Bee Gees and The Little River Band. Later rockers and pop stars include Men At Work, John Farnham, AC/DC, Crowded House, INXS, Midnight Oil, Silverchair, Savage Garden, Yothu Yindi, Powderfinger, Wolfmother and, of course, the "singing budgie" Kylie Minogue.

AN AUSSIE NANNY

Born in Maryborough, Queensland, in 1899, Helen Lyndon Goff went on to write one of the most popular children's stories of all time, which, with the help of Walt Disney, would also become a box office smash that won five Academy Awards in 1965. The book and the film was *Mary Poppins*, featuring the very British nanny, but the book's author (who had reinvented herself as Pamela Lyndon Travers), was one of the few to see the movie who was not enchanted by it. She was upset by the film's portrayal of characters and insisted the book was not written for children.

HAUTE COUTURE

Internationally acclaimed designers such as Collette Dinnigan, Sass & Bide, Wayne Cooper and Carla Zampatti can model their fashions on beautiful Aussie clotheshorses such as Elle Macpherson, Gemma Ward and Miranda Kerr.

MEDIA MAGNATES

Two Australian families have made their mark on national and global media markets — the Murdochs and the Packers. Entrepreneurial Rupert Murdoch, now an American citizen, increased his father Keith's media holdings by buying struggling newspapers and record labels and turning them into successful enterprises. Now, as the chief executive officer of News Corporation, he is one of the world's most powerful media moguls, controlling numerous magazines, newspapers, television stations and movie studios. His success is rivalled in Australia only by the wealthy Packer dynasty, which grew into a media empire under the control of Sir Frank Packer, CEO of Consolidated Press. Murdoch once described him as "the biggest crook in Australian newspapers, but equally he is the cleverest". Upon Sir Frank's death the empire passed to son Kerry and is now under the control of James Packer.

the FACTS!

CHARLES KINGSFORD SMITH was a fearless flyer but he suffered from what he called "aquaphobia" after nearly drowning on Sydney's Bondi Beach as a young boy. In fact, he and a friend were the first people to be rescued by the new Bondi Lifesaving Association on 3 December 1906.

SLIM DUSTY, who was born David Gordon Kirkpatrick near Kempsey, NSW, in 1927, recorded more than 106 country music albums from 1943 until his death in 2003.

CAROLINE CHISHOLM, whose image once graced Australia's $5 note was famous for her philanthropy and efforts to assist poverty-stricken immigrants. Mrs Chisholm established the Female Immigrant's Home in Sydney and also set up a Family Loan Colonisation Society to help poor immigrants. She was known as "The emigrant's friend" and these words are engraved on her tombstone in Northampton, England.

AUSTRALIA'S FIRST ABORIGINAL MP was Neville Bonner, who sat as a Queensland Senator from 1971–1983.

PHILANTHROPIC PROFESSOR Fred Hollows co-founded the Aboriginal Medical Service and was director of the National Trachoma and Eye Health Program. He also helped bring vision to the impoverished in Vietnam, Eritrea and Nepal.

SIR ROBERT HELPMANN was born in Mount Gambier, South Australia, in 1909 and went on to become the nation's most famous ballet dancer. Helpmann partnered Dame Margot Fonteyn and danced with the Royal Ballet for many years.

Sydney AUSTRALIA

Aussie
innovations & inventors

The bionic ear, refrigeration, even the humble ute — all prove that at least a page in the history of invention has to be reserved for some ingenious Australian creations.

the FACTS!

THE SYDNEY General Post Office invented the postcard (above) in October 1875.

HUGH VICTOR McKAY invented the first horse-drawn stripper harvester in 1884 and named it the Sunshine Harvester. The company later merged with Massey–Ferguson.

VEGEMITE (right) was first sold by entrepreneur Fred Walker in 1923. It was made from yeast that was discarded from beer brewing and was described as "pure vegetable extract". At one point, the name was changed to Parwill, using the tacky slogan "If Marmite, Parwill". The name did not last and reverted to Vegemite in the 1930s. American company Kraft bought the product after Walker's death in 1935 and Australia's national food icon remains an American-owned product.

PROFESSOR GRAEME CLARKE developed the bionic ear cochlear implant in the late 1970s.

IN 1915, father and son team Sir William Henry Bragg and Sir William Lawrence Bragg won the Nobel Prize for physics for developing X-ray crystallography, which changed how scientists studied molecular structures. William Lawrence, at 25, was the world's youngest laureate.

AT JUST FOURTEEN years of age, Henry Sutton devised an electronic engine that was later developed by a Belgian man into the "gramme". After 1871, it formed the basis for the electric motors taken up in industry.

SOME INVENTORS OF DEVICES as varied as the winged keel (Ben Lexcen) to Gardisil (Dr Ian Fraser's cervical cancer vaccine) received acclaim for their work. Others — such as David Warren, who invented a prototype black box flight recorder in 1954 — were little known, received little to no financial reward and faded to obscurity, living on only through their creations. Walter Hume, the Australian inventor of the Hume-spun concrete pipe, used in construction around the globe, never quite became a household name, despite the wide application of his invention. Similarly, Lawrence Hargrave, whose experiments with box kites in the 1890s pioneered the Wright Brother's later success, is considered insignificant, and Herbert Lysaught, who conceived the idea of galvanised iron, is a blip in the history books. However, the "Eureka" moments of some wacky inventors have been immortalised in some quintessentially Australian products, such as motor mechanic Lance Hill's 1945 "Hill's Hoist" rotating clothesline, and Lewis Bandt's 1932 "utility" truck, designed to "carry the family to church on Sunday and pigs to market on Monday".

SURE YOU DID!

Edward Davy, the local doctor in Malmsbury, Victoria, was thought to be telling tales when he swore he had invented the telegraph in the 1850s. The honour for its invention was already universally thought to go to two British scientists named Cooke and Wheatstone. However, in 1883, it came to light that Edward Davy had indeed patented the electrical relay system in 1838, however a series of unfortunate events saw him move to Australia just as two English railway companies were set to adopt his invention. Davy left the patent in charge of his father, who sold it to Cooke and Wheatstone in 1847 for just £600. The Society of Telegraph Engineers later added Davy's name to Cooke and Wheatstone's, giving him some credit for his invention.

TOP SECRET STUFF

Twenty-two-year-old Melburnian Louis Brennan invented the deadly self-propelled Brennan Torpedo in his parent's backyard in 1874, and tested it at Hobson's Bay near Melbourne. The Victorian Ministry of Defence, recognising the power of the weapon, part funded the cost of a production model and the torpedo design was later accepted by the British Government, which paid the young man a whopping £110,000. Curiously, the Victorian Government was later denied a request to purchase one of the Brennan Torpedoes by the British Government, who claimed it was too top secret! Brennan went on to lay the foundations for the invention of the monorail and to create a prototype helicopter for the British Royal Air Force.

FLOORED BY FLOREY

Everyone knows that Alexander Fleming discovered *Pencillium notatum* in 1928, but few realise that the true genius behind turning it into the life-saving antibiotics we take for granted belongs to a man described by colleagues as "the bushranger of research"— 1945 Nobel Prize-winner Sir Howard Florey (right). As Professor of Pathology at Oxford University in the 1930s, Florey and his team conducted crucial experiments into the application of penicillin and released the first antibiotics for use on Allied troops in WWII in 1938. Florey was knighted in 1944.

Left to right: Royal Flying Doctor badge; Ironically and tragically Lewis Bandt invented the vehicle that would later be the death of him. He was killed in 1987 while driving a replica ute. The ute (left) remains a popular Australian vehicle.

FLYING DOCTORS

Victorian medical student Clifford Peel first devised the idea of an aerial ambulance for outback patients in 1917 and Presbyterian missionary John Flynn (who became known as Flynn of the Inland) suggested a pedal-operated wireless to help with communication. Engineer Alfred Traeger designed the device, and, combined, the two concepts became the Royal Flying Doctor Service, which covered almost 80% of the continent. Its first flight departed from Cloncurry, north-west Queensland, on 17 May 1928, and it has saved thousands of lives since.

DAVID UNAIPON

Australia's $50 note pays tribute to this prolific inventor, who was also the first published Aboriginal author and was known as "Australia's Leonardo". As well as an improved hand-piece for shearing sheep (1909) he devised a centrifugal motor, a multi-radial wheel and a mechanical propulsion device. In 1914, based on the aerofoil properties of the boomerang, he even made sketches that anticipated the invention of the helicopter.

the FACTS!

IN A LAND where betting is so popular, it figures that the totalisator horse-betting system was devised by George Julius in 1917. Later computer-based betting systems were also Australian made.

LAWN MOWING became considerably easier when Mervyn Victor Richardson conceived the Victa rotary mower in 1952.

STYLE ICONS know that the popularity of the "mini" began here in Australia when English model Jean Shrimpton wore a shockingly short dress to the 1965 Melbourne Cup.

PROLIFIC INVENTOR Ted Both devised the humidicrib, the portable iron lung and the electric scoreboard for the 1956 Melbourne Olympics.

THE OWEN submachine-gun was invented by EE Owen in the 1930s.

NOT SURPRISINGLY, given Australia's predilection for booze, the first wine cask was produced by wine-makers Angove in 1965.

JOHN PAUL WILD created Interscan radio landing equipment for aircraft and Ralph Sarich devised the orbital combustion process engine.

THE GRANNY SMITH Apple, Blue-heeler Cattle Dog and Kelpie Sheep Dog were all first produced in Australia by careful cross-breeding.

WHEN SOUTH AUSTRALIA'S "Pop" Kaisler built a house on top of his 1924 Dodge car, he created the first mobile home.

OTHER EVERYDAY Aussie inventions were notepads (1902), disposable syringes (1949), anti-counterfeit banknotes (1992) and long-wearing contact lenses (1999).

SAVIOURS IN THE SEA

The nation's love affair with sun, surf and sand meant that the establishment of the world's first Lifesaving Club at Sydney's Bondi Beach in 1906 quickly followed the lifting of the ban on daylight bathing in 1902. The Surf Lifesaving reel was also invented in Australia by Mr Lyster Ormsby, captain of the Bondi club. Today, lifesavers (left) remain the volunteer guardian angels of the beaches, cautioning people to swim between the flags and helping those who might otherwise succumb to the sheer power of the surf.

THE ICE MAN COMETH

Editor of the *Geelong Advertiser* James Harrison discovered the concept of refrigeration when he found the ether used to clean printing presses turned the metal cold when it evaporated. Together with Frenchman Eugene Nicolle he set about investigating whether the phenomenon could be used to produce ice and, in 1856, patented the design for the world's first refrigerator. In 1857, he opened the first refrigeration plant on the Barwon River and began creating three tonnes of ice daily. No one in the Northern Hemisphere was interested in purchasing his invention at the time and he later went broke in 1861 as people were content to keep using ice boxes stocked with ice imported from the US in the cargo hold of ships.

ONE BIG CLASSROOM

In June 1951, children in remote Alice Springs began to be taught via radio in the School of the Air, transmitted from the Royal Flying Doctor Base. Adelaide Miethke began the school, which conducts lessons via two-way radio. Using radio, the children interact with classmates who are also isolated on remote outback properties. The school has no State boundaries, so children enrolled in the Alice Springs School of the Air may be from any State. In total, about 3 million children are taught in the school, which extends over 4 million km². Recent technological advances have allowed the School of the Air to incorporate satellite technology, intranet, internet, fax and telephone services into the curriculum.

A bunch of dags
— our quirky humour

Above: An Aussie "ankle biter" (kid) pretending to ride his dog and generally playing "silly buggers".

the FACTS!

MOST AUSTRALIAN STATES have a mildly derogatory nickname bestowed on them by other Australians. Queenslanders are Cane Toads or Bananabenders, South Australians are Crow-eaters, Western Australians are Sandgropers, New South Welshmen are Cockroaches, and Victorians are Mexicans, because they are south of the border.

GOVERNOR BRIDGES told men at the annual dinner for the Limbless Soldiers Association in Adelaide in 1924 to "keep on kicking". It was a joke, not an oversight, because he lost his own leg in the war.

AFTER FEDERATION, bickering between NSW and Victoria over the site for the nation's capital was so intense that the New South Wales' premier threatened to withdraw from Federation altogether. Prime Minister Alfred Deakin's rebuttal was to advise his secretary to, "Tell him to go to hell — three pages".

IN 1906, AUTHOR Edward Dyson wrote about the typical Australian man, "The more he learns [about women] the more he puts his confidence in beer".

IN AN 1896 example of bureaucratic farce, Sydney police considered a proposal to wear rubber-soled shoes so they could sneak up on offenders!

A COMMON Australian joke is to call people who have red hair Bluey.

Technically, a dag is a small piece of faeces that dangles from the woolly back end of a sheep, but in Australia the word is used endearingly to refer to a person who is being silly or is not very sophisticated.

AUSTRALIANS ARE RENOWNED for their laconic sense of humour and tendency to see the funny side to even the most dire circumstance. It is probably a habit borne out of the difficult pioneering past when, as the saying goes, "You had to laugh or you would cry". The national humour also typically shows a cheeky disregard for class or culture, with somewhat disparaging nicknames being "affectionately" granted to even the most high-ranking dignitaries. Australia's first Prime Minister, Edmund Barton, was even given the nickname "Tosspot Toby" because he was known to enjoy a drink or two. Similarly, wartime Prime Minister Billy Hughes was known as the "Little Digger" and long-serving PM John Howard as "Little Johnny". One of the best examples of the fine line drawn between insult and humorous "ribbing" (teasing) is the use of the word "b*stard", which is often bestowed affectionately, as in "Bill, you old b*stard, how the hell are you?", much to the consternation of those not used to such an impolite figure of speech.

Above: Children "muck around" on the sand in front of Brighton's (Vic) vivid beach houses.

Below, left to right: Cheeky "wags" frequently "take the mickey" out of everyday objects, such as road signs, by adding their own humorous amendments, such as graffiti-ing legs onto a roadbump sign to create a before and after vision of a cassowary; Cartoonist Ken Maynard created the slanting, dilapidated Ettamogah Pub and its ocker, blue-singleted inhabitants in the 1950s and it was not long before enterprising individuals constructed three-dimensional versions to serve as tourist attractions. This one is found at Aussie World at Palmview on Queensland's Sunshine Coast.

Tongue-in-cheek Art
Australia abounds with wacky sculptures that raise a laugh, such as the farmer and his cow (far left), the optical illusion of "Nessie" on The Strand, Townsville, (left), and the "struck down" ute (below).

THE BIGGER THE BETTER

Why Australians are fascinated with big things and build one in just about every tiny town is a mystery. Perhaps it is a consequence of Australia being such a big country, or perhaps, as cynics suggest, it is purely to give the many tourists who pull into these backwaters something to spend their money on apart from petrol. At any rate, they are big buck-spinners and few can resist dropping a few dollars on a Big Barramundi beer cooler in the Daintree. The Big Banana, near Coffs Harbour, was probably the first oversized object, but stranger ones have followed, such as the Big Winch at Coober Pedy, the Big Milkshake Container in Kyabram, and the Big Worm in Bass, Victoria, which offers the not-to-be-missed opportunity to crawl through a 100-m-long replica worm's stomach! The Big Cigar in Churchill, Vic, honours British cigar-lover Winston Churchill, and the Big Mosquito in Hexham would certainly leave a big bite. Ballina has a Big Prawn, Nambour a Big Pineapple and a Big Cow, and Glenrowan a Giant Ned Kelly. Once you've driven around seeing them all, you might want to visit Buronga, home of the Big Wine Cask.

Above, top to bottom: The 17-m-high Big Lobster in Kingston, South Australia; The freakishly animate Big Rocking Horse at Gumeracha, South Australia.

the FACTS!

POOR QUEENSLAND bears the brunt of many a joke at the expense of the other States, but the following true event did little to help the State's reputation. In 1873, two men in Queensland found a man hanging but still alive and hurried to notify the police at a station several hours away. Police arrived as quickly as they could, but the man, whom they had failed to cut down, was, not surprisingly, dead.

ANOTHER STRANGE but true incident occurred when an inmate from Kew Asylum was entrusted with driving a van full of beer and refreshments to fellow inmates working in the paddock. Instead, he drove it to Bendigo and went on a two week bender. Authorities figured he would be quickly caught because the van had KEW ASYLUM emblazoned on the side, but he had scratched off the ASY so people thought it belonged to a Chinese trader named Kew Lum.

ECCENTRIC WILLIAM KING — the "Flying Pieman" clocked up a number of bizarre records well before the Guiness Book of Records was established. His feats included picking 100 cobs of corn (each 1 m apart) in 53 minutes and carrying a 4 kg goat and a 5.5 kg weight from a pub in Sydney to one in Parramatta and back (about 46 km) in 6 hours and 48 minutes.

ACROSS THE DITCH

Australians have a habit of good-naturedly teasing New Zealanders across the Tasman for their supposed familiarity with sheep. However, it is Australia that is the true sheep capital of the world and about 140 million "woolly baa-baas" — around twenty per person — in Australia produce 70% of the world's wool. The rivalry between Aussies and the Kiwis "across the ditch" is well known, but in truth most Aussies think fondly of Kiwis as their Antipodean cousins; whether that sentiment is reciprocated is another matter.

Right: Sheep own the road on some of the "long paddock" stock routes and unfenced roads in Australia's outback. Sheep jokes and cracks about "Noo Zuhlunders'" accents remain the source of ongoing banter between Australians and New Zealanders.

Talk the
hindlegs off a donkey

Above: The "milko" has delivered to the steps of the Opera House.

the FACTS!

SHEILA is a common Irish girls' name that was originally applied in Australia to Irish girls in the same way that "Paddy" or "Mick" was applied to Irish males. Over time, it came to be used to refer to females in general. Most women now consider its use sexist, especially in the context of derogatory jibes such as, "You throw like a sheila". But usually it is cheekily employed by Australian men to "stir up" their partners or female friends.

"DRONGO" is colloquial slang for an idiot and comes from a racehorse in the 1920s that never won a race.

"CLAYTON'S" REFERS to anything that will never be or has never been a reality. Thus a "clayton's tax break". The word is taken from the advertising for Clayton's soft drink, in which actor Jack Thompson said it was "the drink I have when I'm not having a drink".

AFL PLAYER Roy Cazaly was renowned for his high marks (catches). Crowds used to shout, "Up there, Cazaly!" when he leapt for the ball and the cry was later taken up by Australian soldiers as they went over the trenches in WWII.

TYPICALLY, AUSSIES came to know the cameleers that worked in Central Australia as "Ghans" — short for Afghans — and even named the Ghan railway, which replaced the ships of the desert, in their honour. Many of the men were actually from Pakistan, Turkey, Iran or Egypt.

In 1923, author HL Mencken wrote that the Australian vocabulary is "heavy with loans from America, but there are also some picturesque native inventions". In fact, a lot of Australian slang words originated in Cockney London, and others are due to the Aussie tendency to shorten or slur words. Aboriginal words enhance the language and a strong Irish heritage gives most Australians the "gift of the gab".

THE "FLASH" COCKNEY LANGUAGE of rhyming slang, which was first used by thieves as a code to avoid arrest in the streets of London's East End, was brought to Australia with the First Fleet and continued to grow and expand as more and more British convicts were shipped to Australia. Thus, the wife became "trouble and strife", the pub "rubbedy dub", the road "the frog and toad", a shark "Noah's Ark" and sauce the unappetising "dead horse". New phrases were coined to describe purely Australian situations, hence to "have a Captain Cook" meant look, "Joe Blake" meant snake, "steak and kidney" became Sydney, a "Dad and Dave" was a shave, and to have a "Barry Crocker" was to have a "shocker" or give a poor performance.

Above: A backyard dunny. The term is a shortened form of the English word "dunnekin"— a building where dung was stored.

A QUICKIE ON THE LINGO

Why use a long word when a short one will do the job? Australians are known for shortening words by adding "o", "ie", or "zza" to the end. Just about every Aussie knows a Robbo (Robert) or a Kazza (Karen), enjoys a biccie (biscuit) with their smoko (smoke break), or a ciggie (cigarette) before brekkie (breakfast), and a coldie (cold beer) with their barbie (barbecue). Their rubbish is collected by the garbo (garbage man), they chat to the cabbie (cab driver), lay a bet with a bookie (bookmaker) and curse the Aussie pollies (politicians) when they get together with the rellies (relatives). A quickie can apply to anything done quickly, but be careful — it can also have other, rather rude connotations.

THAT'S NOT A TINNIE, *THIS* IS A TINNIE!

As if Australian slang isn't confusing enough for foreigners, there are a few words that have multiple meanings. Aussie blokes might set out on the weekend for a fishing trip in the tinnie (aluminium dinghy, right) but they might also pack a few tinnies (beer in aluminium cans) in the Esky® for the trip. Instead of tinnies, they might take stubbies (beer in short, squat bottles) and sit there drinking it in just their stubbies (short shorts)!

THE UNSEXY THONG

Thongs (above) are an Aussie icon, but when mentioned to Americans or the British, the humble "flip flops" as they are known in other parts of the world, are invariably mistaken for a far more attractive piece of female intimate apparel — the G-string (or thong brief). Aussies are proud of their casual national footwear and can be seen wearing them just about anywhere that dress regulations permit, including the beach, surf club, shops and, sometimes, the local watering hole (pub).

TELLING FURPHIES

The Furphy horse-drawn water cart was invented by John Furphy & Sons in Shepparton, Victoria, in the late 1800s and used on battlefields during WWI. Men naturally gathered near the water carts, and the "furphies", as they were known, became places where rumours were spread. By 1915, furphies came to mean lies or incorrect rumours. Incidentally, John Furphy's brother, Joseph, also found fame when he wrote the novel *Such is Life* under the pen name of Tom Collins in 1903.

ROOS LOOSE

Inventive similes and metaphors are liberally scattered throughout "Strine" (the tongue-in-cheek name for Australian English, which is a drawled version of 'Stralian). If someone is very busy they are "flat out like a lizard drinking", something messy looks "like a dog's breakfast" and something not very useful is "useless as pockets on a singlet" and you "need it like a hole in the head". It's enough to send you "troppo" (mad), in which case you'd have "roos loose in the top paddock".

BARCOO BANTER

The Barcoo River in western Queensland is definitely outback and the region has lent its name to some quaint phrases such as "Barcoo salute", a movement to shoo flies away from the eyes, and "Barcoo bun", a small damper. A type of diarrhoea became known as "Barcoo sickness", and the connotation eventually led to it being used as a polite way to refer to a rude bodily function, for example, "He gives me the barcoos".

THE GREAT AUSSIE YARN

"Telling a yarn" is the ability to spin a good tale, but "having a yarn" usually means having a chat. Strangely, Swiss-born Louis de Rougemont goes down in history as the greatest yarn spinner on Earth. He managed to convince newspaper editors in London that he had spent 30 years living as a cannibal chief among Australian Aborigines, where he built a house of pearl shells, sent messages home on a fleet of pelicans and rode on giant sea turtles. Eventually, his preposterous fabrications, such as "wombats flying off in clouds at sunset" brought him undone and in October 1898 he was revealed to be Henri Grin, a Swiss man with a very vivid imagination. Grin was not at all put out by being discovered; instead he held lectures selling himself as the "Greatest Liar on Earth". Most yarns revolve around embellishing a story to make it more amusing or dramatic and old men and bushies are usually the most accomplished yarners.

the FACTS!

THE ESKY® (above) was first manufactured by Malleys in the 1950s and by the 1970s all of these portable ice-boxes became known by this proprietary name. Coincidentally, the Kiwis, rather quaintly, call them "chilly bins".

"DINKUM" and its derivative "dinky-di" can mean honest, truthful or reasonable, and "true blue" also means the real deal or dinkum.

THE "BUSH TELEGRAPH" was used to describe the way Aborigines communicated using smoke signals and clapping sticks. It may also be used to describe gossip or word of mouth in the outback.

"BLUDGER" is commonly used in Australia for someone who shirks work or takes advantage of someone else, but it was originally used to describe a pimp who lived off a prostitute's immoral earnings. Australians may use it to ask, "Can I bludge a smoke off you?"

"AVAGOYERMUG" (have a go, you mug) and "Caaarn!" (come on) are rallying cries used to encourage sporting teams in Australia.

A STRANGE AND RECENT addition to Australian speech is the confusing and contradictory habit of initially answering a query with "yeah no". This figure of speech often follows a compliment and some linguists believe it is the Aussie way of filling an otherwise awkward gap in a conversation, or politely acknowledging a query before answering in the negative. An example might be a journalist asking a sports star, "Has it sunk in that you're the world champion?", to be answered, "Yeah no, I just tried my best you know."

Above: Fireworks over the Swan River, Perth, WA, usher in the New Year.

Events, festivals
& celebrations

Throughout the year, Australia's towns and cities come alive with various festivals and events. Some are national days of celebration or commemoration, others are obscure, riotous festivals where camels or cane toads race or people judge boats built out of beer cans. Either way, people throng the streets to enjoy the colour and the ceremony.

the
FACTS!

THAT AUSTRALIANS will bet on anything is borne out by some of the wackier events held throughout Australia, such as lizard races on the Paroo Track at Eulo, Qld, each August. Incidentally, a plaque at the track states it is also where Destructo, a champion racing cockroach, met his fate after beating Wooden Head, a champion lizard.

IN ANOTHER EXAMPLE that Australians will bet on anything, two-up is a game of chance in which two pre-decimal pennies are thrown in the air and people bet on one of three possible outcomes — two tails, two heads or one of each. It is traditionally played on Anzac Day and "Come in spinner" is the term used to ask the coin spinner to throw the two pennies in the air.

IN THE "WILD WEST" of Australia's outback, rodeos (below), which usually include events such as bronco riding, wood-chopping competitions and cattle drafting displays, give outback folk a chance to kick up their heels.

EVERY YEAR, Australians enjoy a public holiday for Labour Day — few realise it commemorates the eight-hour working day and that Australia was the first country in the world to introduce this workplace reform.

A HOLIDAY COUNTRY

Australia's two major national celebrations are Australia Day on 26 January (the day the First Fleet landed) and Anzac Day on 25 April each year. Both honour the spirit of what it means to be Australian, although the former is a joyous celebration and the latter is a day for poignant reflection and paying tribute to those who fought for this country in all conflicts. Aside from Anzac Day and Australia Day, each Australian State celebrates at least three other public holidays throughout the year (including the Queen's Birthday), as well as the Christmas and Easter break and New Year's Day. Australians make the most of their long weekends and flock to the beaches and national parks to picnic, camp, boat, swim and fish. Some holidays are such big events that, even in 1896, author Nat Gould wrote "[What the Australian] requires is the day before to prepare for the holiday, then the holiday itself, and then the remainder of the week to get over it". The party atmosphere that surrounds most public holidays means that sentiment is still very true today.

Above: **A decorated veteran marches in the Anzac Day parade. Anzac Day is reserved for remembering lost friends and paying respects to the servicemen and women of Australia.**

Below: **Surf lifesaving carnivals, triathalons and iron man/woman events gather crowds year round.**

Above, top to bottom: **Fred Brophy's Boxing Troupe has been entertaining crowds at outback events for decades and anyone brave enough or silly enough is invited to step up and challenge one of his fighters for a prize; Tiny Birdsville in western Queensland usually has a population of 100, but during the Birdsville Races in September an influx of visitors from all over the world rush to the town's only pub.**

CULTURE & ARTS

Along with Australia Day festivities, each State holds numerous smaller arts, comedy and cultural festivals, including writers' festivals, multicultural festivals, historic festivals and music festivals. Floral extravaganzas are showcased during Perth's Wildflower Festival and Canberra's Floriade Festival, both in September. Melbourne's International Comedy Festival is sure to tickle a funny bone, and the Sydney Film Festival is attended by locals and celebrities alike. Tasmania celebrates the Ten Days on the Island festival biennially.

Above, left to right: A float celebrates the Australian film *Priscilla Queen of the Desert* in an Australia Day parade in Brisbane, Qld; Brisbane's Riverfire celebration in September; Bush balladeers entertain the crowds.

THE DAY THE NATION STOPS

Every year since 1861, at 3 pm Eastern Standard Time on the first Tuesday in November, the nation stops and holds its breath for the few minutes it takes some of the world's quickest horses to gallop the 3200-m Melbourne Cup at Flemington. Cup day is a public holiday in Melbourne, but this "race that stops a nation", as it is known, is celebrated in all States and most Aussies "have a flutter" (place a bet), engage in office sweepstakes and wear elaborate hats to replicate the famed fashions on the field. Carbine and Phar Lap are the most famous cup winners, but in 2005 the plucky little mare Makybe Diva became the first horse to win the Cup three times, winning consecutive races in 2003, 2004 and 2005 and earning her spot in the Australian Racing Museum and Hall of Fame.

WACKY REGATTAS

A sarcastic bit of Northern Territory fun is the Henley-on-Todd Regatta in late August/early September, where bottomless, foot-propelled "yachts" are raced in the dry sandy bed of the Todd River. The first regatta was held in 1962 and now draws spectators from around the world. The Beer Can Regatta (left), held off Mindil Beach in Darwin as part of the Darwin Festival is also a fun "boat race" where boats constructed out of beer cans are set afloat.

the FACTS!

THE KERNEWEK LOWENDER
Cornish Festival held in the Copper Triangle towns around Burra, SA, celebrates their Cornish heritage.

THE SMALL TOWN of Goomeri in Queensland holds an annual Pumpkin Festival featuring a competition whereby pumpkins are rolled down a hill, with the fastest taking the crown. The organisers caution entrants that oblong-shaped butternut pumpkins traditionally do not perform well.

THE SYDNEY GAY AND LESBIAN MARDI GRAS began in 1978 when a 1000-strong crowd marched down Oxford Street to mark International Gay Solidarity Day. The march was marred by skirmishes with police, which added to the marchers' determination to do it again the following year and the Mardi Gras was born. Today, it draws thousands of homosexual and straight supporters from around the globe to Sydney each February. It is regarded as a cheeky celebration not only of the gay and lesbian lifestyle, but also of Australia's democratic right to be yourself and express yourself individually. Floats poke fun at political and public figures, and marching boys show off their enviable bodies to the world.

SIX OUTDOOR STAGES pumping to the sounds of more than 35 musical groups from more than twenty countries are found at WOMADelaide, South Australia's three-day world music festival in March.

OTHER MUSIC FESTIVALS are the Woodford Folk Festival at Woodford (Qld) in December, the East Coast Blues and Roots Festival at Byron Bay (NSW) over Easter, Splendour in the Grass, and the Big Day Out, which visits most capital cities.

Good sports
— a national love affair

Above: Mackay-born sprinter Cathy Freeman wins the gold medal in the Womens 400 m final at the Olympic Games in Sydney, 2000.

the FACTS!

IN 1887, Aboriginal sprinter Bobby McDonald brought the runner's crouch start to the world's notice.

JOHN WING, a 17-year-old apprentice carpenter, wrote to the organisers of the Melbourne 1956 Olympics suggesting that the athletes should not walk in their national teams for the closing ceremony but should walk together to signify "their common humanity and unity in sport". The idea was adopted and John Wing was honoured for his contribution when the Australian Institute of Sport was opened at Bruce, Canberra, in 1981.

SINCE THE SOCCEROOS qualified for the 2006 World Cup, soccer is enjoying a comeback in Australia. The Australian women's soccer team, the Matildas, have also enjoyed great success.

MOTORCYCLIST Wayne Gardner was the first non-American to win the World Championship in 1987 and is said to have broken every bone in his body over his career.

IN 1988, Sydney's Kay Cottee became the first woman to complete a solo navigation of the world.

"Every Australian worships the Goddess of Sport" wrote E Kinglake in 1891 and while it may not be true of every Australian, it is true of a majority.

SPORT IS A NATIONAL PASTIME, a way to spend our leisure time (either as a spectator or participant) and a mark of our determination to rise above and beyond other nations and be at our best. From beach volleyball to football codes to motorbike racing, just about every sport has a fan base in this country.

OLYMPIC GLORY

In 1956, Melbourne became the first city in the Southern Hemisphere to host the Olympic Games. Unfortunately, Egypt, Iraq, Lebanon, China, Spain, the Netherlands and Switzerland all chose to boycott the games in protest over various political disputes with other countries, but that probably only made it easier for Australian athletes to win thirteen highly coveted gold medals. In 2000, Sydney also basked in Olympic glory. Australia has also had much success in the Commonwealth Games, which it has hosted numerous times, and takes great delight in thrashing the "Mother Country".

SUPER FISH

While Australia's strength in cricket, rugby and international meets is well known, it is in the pool that the nation's athletes really dominate. Swimming sensations include "Boy" Charlton, Murray Rose, "Fanny" Durack, Hayley Lewis, Shane Gould, Ian "Thorpedo" Thorpe, Kieren Perkins and Susie "Madame Butterfly" O'Neill. Dawn Fraser is arguably the most famous, having won eight Olympic medals and set numerous world records. Many of Australia's award-winning swimmers live and train at the Australian Institute of Sport in Canberra.

Above: The Gold Coast SuperGP entices throngs of "petrol heads" to Surfers Paradise to watch the supercars.

Above: Cadel Evans began his career as a mountain biker, placing seventh at the Sydney 2000 Olympics, before switching to road bikes.

Above: Beach volleyball is a fun pastime around the country, but is now also an Olympic sport.

Above: The Basketballer sculpture by Dominique Sutton outside the Australian Institute of Sport at Bruce, Canberra, honours our Paralympic athletes.

AERIAL PING PONG

Australian Football, or Aussie Rules, was invented in the 1850s and is a mix of other football codes. It comprises eighteen players on each team kicking an oval ball around an oval field that is 165 m long and 137 m wide. The aim is to kick the ball through the goalposts, of which there are four, two at the front and two smaller, outer goalposts — if the ball passes only through the outer goalposts, the goal is known as a "behind".

Because it involves a lot of jumping and kicking, AFL is sometimes condescendingly referred to as "aerial ping-pong" by those that prefer the other football codes of Rugby League, Rugby Union or Soccer.

AMERICA'S CUP VICTORY

For more than 21 years, Australia had lofty ambitions to win the America's Cup. In 1983, Perth entrepreneur Alan Bond's yacht *Australia II,* which had been famously fitted with Ben Lexcen's revolutionary winged keel, finally wrenched the cup out of American hands. It was the first time the cup had been won by anyone outside of America, smashing a 132-year record.

ROACHES VS CANE TOADS

One of the most eagerly anticipated events is the State of Origin Rugby League series when the "Cockroaches" (NSW) and the "Cane Toads" (Qld) play three games a year in a fight for State supremacy.

the FACTS!

GREAT AUSTRALIAN BOXER
Les Darcy won his first professional fight at the tender age of fourteen and had 22 straight victories from 1915–1917. Controversially, he left Australia to avoid conscription and fought in America. Marrickville-born Jeff Fenech is another acclaimed pugilist, wining three world titles in three different weight categories.

ROD LAVER, the "Rockhampton Rocket", was the first Australian to win the Grand Slam tennis tournament. Other tennis greats include Margaret Court, Pat Cash, Evonne Goolagong Cawley, Ken Rosewall and Lleyton Hewitt, who was the youngest male player to be crowned world number one.

RUNNER RON CLARKE, the final torchbearer at the Melbourne Olympics, collapsed and nearly died on the track at the Mexico City Olympics. It was discovered he had a heart condition. He broke at least 17 world records over his career.

DON BRADMAN was the first Aussie to have his image on an Australian postage stamp.

TIPSY RUN

Each Christmas Day or Australia Day, you can bet that families everywhere are dusting off a tennis ball and setting up stumps for a game of backyard or beach cricket. These casual cricket matches are usually played with the lenient rules of "tipsy run" (where if the ball touches the bat the batter must run, but possibly so called because a beer always goes down well while fielding). Another rule is that a child batter cannot get out for a duck, and not abiding by this rule is, well, "just not cricket". Despite the relaxed rules of Aussies at play, Australians take their cricket very seriously and many cricketers are regarded as sporting superstars. Legendary batsman Don Bradman, born in Cootamundra, New South Wales, in 1908, is considered the world's greatest cricketer. He made an incredible 271 centuries and captained Australia for more than twelve years. His career test average was 99.94 runs per innings. Bradman was knighted in 1949 and died in Adelaide in 2001 at the age of 92. Other famous Australian cricketers are the moustached Merv Hughes, batsman and captain Ricky Ponting, and spin bowler and legendary troublemaker Shane Warne.

Left: Don Bradman statue outside Adelaide Oval.

Aussie exports,
edibles & economy

the FACTS!

THE FIRST EXPORTS from Australia were cedar logs, which were cut from the Hawkesbury River area and shipped on the *Experiment* on 28 November 1795.

THE AUSTRALIAN DOLLAR was only floated on the world foreign exchange market in 1983. Before then, the Reserve Bank of Australia set the Aussie dollar's value against the US dollar daily.

FOSTER'S LAGER was produced in Victoria in 1887 and became prominent in the 1960s and 70s. It is now exported to more than 150 countries around the globe.

THE ONLY BUSH TUCKER exported in large quantities are Macadamia nuts (below), which are native to Australia.

AUSTRALIA EXPORTS eucalyptus and acacia seed worth $9 million each year to plantations in 40 countries around the globe.

AUSTRALIA IS one of the world's largest wine exporters, exporting more wine to the United Kingdom than France does.

MINING AND ENERGY are Australia's primary export industries, with the largest demand from Asia. Australia ranks in the top five globally for the production of coal, iron ore, lead, gold and diamonds.

When Donald Horne wrote of Australia as "The Lucky Country" in 1964, he actually meant it as a criticism, saying that the nation was "a lucky country, run by second-rate people who share its luck". His book criticised the Australia of the 1960s, which he felt was lucky rather than "smart".

TODAY, THE PHRASE has been accepted literally, and the irony with which it was intended has been overlooked. Most Australians concede that we are indeed the lucky country, where people enjoy democracy, freedom and economic stability based on a healthy export in natural resources, but we're also learning to use that "luck" more wisely. Australia is still one of the largest wool, wheat and beef producers in the world. It is also one of the largest mining nations globally and trades in bauxite, zinc and the more controversial coal and uranium. However, Australia is also a nation intent on channelling funds into research and technology, and some of Australia's discoveries in medicine and technology rival the biggest breakthroughs in the world. Services and technology account for around 80% of the country's economic activity. Added to that is a strong tourism market with many millions flocking to the continent each year to visit the Great Barrier Reef, the outback, the beaches and the cosmopolitan capital cities, with some tourists even spending more than a year travelling the continent.

Below: **Tourism helps keep the Australian economy strong.**

TRUE BLUE TUCKER

In reality, along with Indigenous bush tucker, only two dishes can be considered truly Australian — lamingtons and the pavlova (and the Kiwis dispute the last). Chef Bert Sachse is said to have created the first pavlova at the Esplanade Hotel in Perth in 1935, naming it after Russian ballerina Anna Pavlova, who stayed at the hotel during the Australian leg of her tour. The lamington, a finger of sponge cake covered in chocolate icing and coconut, first appeared in Australian recipe books in 1909. It is named after Queensland's Governor from 1895–1901, Charles Cochrane-Baillie, Baron Lamington.

Golden syrup, rolled oats and desiccated coconut are the major ingredients in the famed Anzac biscuits, which were sent to Australian troops during World War II and now remain a favourite Australian biscuit.

A SOCIAL SAFETY NET

Today, Australia enjoys one of the highest living standards in the world — some might say too high, as interest rate rises to curb inflation push the Great Australian Dream of home ownership out of reach. However, the country has not always enjoyed this measure of affluence. In 1929, when the American stock market plummeted, Australia was plunged into the Great Depression. Because Australian trade was heavily reliant on the export of primary goods and on funds borrowed from overseas, at the depression's worst, in 1932, almost 40% of workers were unemployed.

As the depression worsened, the government was forced to introduce sustenance payments, known as "susso", in the form of food coupons. Some States also offered relief work. Now, Australia has a "safety net" of social services for those who are temporarily out of work or those who require assistance due to illness or incapacitation.

Life-changing
laws & policies

The Australian government follows Britain's Westminster system combined with some elements of the United State's congressional system. Britain does not have a constitution, but the Australian system, like that of America, does. People must vote in a referendum to approve proposed changes to the constitution.

AUSTRALIA IS OFFICIALLY the Commonwealth of Australia and is governed by a constitutional monarchy. Queen Elizabeth II is the head of State, represented by the governor-general. The prime minister is the head of government, the leader of the political party that holds the majority of parliamentarians in federal parliament. Federal parliament is made up of two houses — the House of Representatives (the lower house) and the Senate (upper house). Each State and Territory also has its own parliament and local councils, but federal laws override State laws if there is a conflict. MPs and councillors have a duty to serve the people of their electorate.

WHITE AUSTRALIA POLICY

Australia's first federal parliament almost unanimously agreed to keep Australia white and passed the *Immigration Restriction Act* and the *Pacific Islanders Labourers Act* to achieve those ends. The act was overturned in 1959, when the Liberal–Country coalition government allowed for admission, regardless of race, to the wives and children of Australian citizens and to other "distinguished and highly qualified people". In 1972, the Labor government also adopted a policy based on "the avoidance of discrimination on any grounds of race or colour of skin".

ABORIGINAL RIGHTS

Australians have voted "no" to far more changes to the constitution in referendums than they have passed (just 8 of 44 had been passed in 2007), leading Sir John Walsh to famously quip in 1965, "You couldn't introduce free beer by referendum." However, on 27 May 1967, more than 90% of Australians voted to allow Aborigines to be counted on the national census. This extended voting rights to all Aborigines, not just those who had "sufficiently developed the attributes of civilisation" as previously granted on 3 March 1949. The outcome of the

Mabo v The State of Queensland case in 1992 rejected the concept of *terra nullius*, granting the Meriam people native title to traditional lands. In 1993, the Keating government passed the *Native Title Act*, which allowed for the establishment of a tribunal to process native title claims.

REPUBLICAN RUMBLINGS

Whether or not Australia should become a republic has been discussed from as early as 1850, when the Australian League campaigned for a republican form of government. On 6 November 1999, Australians voted on the issue — it was, not surprisingly given the country's track record in referendums, defeated. Australians are still very divided on the republic debate.

STRANGE LAWS WE LOST

Over the years, obscure laws have also been changed. On 3 February 1871, South Australia made it legal for a man to marry his dead wife's sister (it was the first British colony to allow this). In 1874, fifteen people in Sydney were arrested for playing cricket on the Sabbath. They were released with a caution but the laws stipulated that they could be held in stocks for breaking the fourth commandment.

the FACTS!

IN 1965, Charles Perkins and a group of students undertook a "Freedom Ride" throughout New South Wales campaigning to end segregation between white Australians and Aborigines in swimming pools and cinemas.

IN SEPTEMBER 1947, the Federal Arbitration Court ruled Australians should work a 40-hour week.

AUSTRALIAN WOMEN WERE first allowed to vote in South Australia in 1894. Other States did not extend women the vote until 1902. The first woman to enter parliament was Edith Cowan, in Western Australia, who was elected in 1921.

VOTING IS COMPULSORY for all Australian citizens over the age of eighteen and is seen as a privilege and a responsibility.

ON 16 DECEMBER 1972, women were awarded equal pay under the Commonwealth Arbitration Commission.

THE IDEA OF A "LIVING WAGE" — the basics required to support a labourer, his wife and three children led to the formation of a "minimum wage". The living wage was defined by Justice Higgins in the Harvester judgement of 1907 and was about 42 shillings at the time.

AUSTRALIA'S HIGHEST COURT is the High Court in Canberra.

Above: The 6-metre-high statue of Ned Kelly in Glenrowan, the scene of the infamous final shoot out.

the FACTS!

THE AUSTRALIAN GOVERNMENT is split into three "arms" — legislative, executive and judicial. The prime minister and his ministers (the Cabinet) make up the legislative branch and develop the policies and bills that, if passed, will be legislated. The judicial arm (the federal court system) interprets and upholds the law. The executive branch includes government ministers, agencies and the members of the Australian Public Service, who act as advisory bodies and administer the legislation at a ground roots level.

AUSTRALIANS ARE FREE to follow whichever religion, if any, they choose. Freedom of speech and association mean that Australian citizens can gather together in peaceful demonstrations or form organisations that enable them to express themselves.

THE PLEDGE NEW CITIZENS make when their request for citizenship is approved is as follows: *From this time forward, under God* (people can choose to omit the words "under God" if they wish) / *I pledge my loyalty to Australia and its people/Whose democratic beliefs I share/Whose rights and liberties I respect, and/Whose laws I will uphold and obey.*

A quick quiz
for citizens

In 2007, the government introduced a "citizenship test" to help those wishing to become Australian citizens learn about the nation's history, culture and values. How much do you know about Australia? All of the answers to our quiz, below, are found at the bottom of the page.

Q.1 When did "Advance Australia Fair" become the national anthem?

Q.2 What two animals are shown on the Australian Coat of Arms?

Q.3 What is Australia's longest river?

Q.4 What is Australia's highest mountain?

Q.5 Where and when did Captain Cook claim Australia's east coast as British land?

Q.6 How many ships were in the First Fleet?

Q.7 What responsibility is considered a democratic right and is compulsory for Australians over the age of 18?

Q.8 In what year did Federation occur?

Q.9 What "living fossils" are found at Hamelin Pool, Western Australia?

Q.10 Who is Australia's only Nobel Prize winning author?

Q.11 Aboriginal culture is the _____ continuous culture on Earth?

Q.12 When were Australian women allowed to vote federally?

Q.13 What is the highest court in Australia?

Q.14 What constellation appears on the Australian flag?

Q.15 What State received Australia's last shipment of convicts in 1868?

Q.16 Who were the "emancipists"?

Q.17 What is an Akubra®?

Q.18 Which famous German explorer vanished in 1848 and has never been found?

Q.19 What public holiday commemorates the introduction of the eight-hour work day?

Q.20 Who led Australia's first polar expedition?

Q.21 What is the largest structure in the world built by living organisms?

Q.22 Australia's system of government is officially a c_____ m_____?

Q.23 The world's largest sand island is found in Australia; what is its name?

Q.24 What is the governor-general's role?

Q.25 The Platypus and the echidna are both mammals known as ___?

Q.26 What is Tasmania's faunal emblem?

Q.27 What is the slang term for one of Australia's most talked about values that promises equal opportunity for all?

Q.28 Who wrote the ballad *Waltzing Matilda*?

Q.29 Which prime minister was famously "sacked" on 11 November 1975?

Q.30 What is commemorated on 25 April?

Q.31 What were Ned Kelly's last words?

Q.32 What is a bunyip?

Q.33 Dawn Fraser is a famous _____?

Q.34 Who was known as the "Lone Eagle"?

Q.35 Who won the Nobel Prize for his work creating antibiotics?

Q.36 What was Phar Lap?

Q.37 What sporting event did *Australia II* win in 1983?

Q.38 Why is Sir Donald Bradman famous?

Q.39 Australia is the world's largest exporter of ____ and ____?

Q.40 What change to the constitution did Australians pass by a more than 90% majority in 1967?

QUIZ ANSWERS

A.1 In 1984, before then *God Save the Queen* was the anthem. **A.2** The kangaroo and Emu. **A.3** The Murray. **A.4** Mt Kosciuszko. **A.5** Possession Island in Queensland on 22 August 1770. **A.6** Eleven. **A.7** Voting in elections. **A.8** In 1901. **A.9** Stromatolites. **A.10** Patrick White. **A.11** Oldest. **A.12** From 1902 (but from 1894 in SA). **A.13** The High Court. **A.14** The Southern Cross. **A.15** Western Australia. They arrived in Fremantle on the *Hougoumont*. **A.16** Freed convicts who argued with free settlers (exclusives) about who should be allowed to vote and own land in the early days of settlement. **A.17** A type of hat. **A.18** Ludwig Leichhardt. **A.19** Labour Day or Eight Hours Day. **A.20** Sir Douglas Mawson. **A.21** The Great Barrier Reef. **A.22** Constitutional monarchy. **A.23** Fraser Island. **A.24** The Queen's representative Head of State in Australia. **A.25** Monotremes. **A.26** The Tasmanian Devil. **A.27** A "fair go". **A.28** AB "Banjo" Paterson. **A.29** Gough Whitlam. **A.30** Anzac Day. **A.31** Such is life. **A.32** A beast from Aboriginal mythology. **A.33** Swimmer. **A.34** Aviator Bert Hinkler. **A.35** Howard Florey. **A.36** A champion racehorse. **A.37** The America's Cup. **A.38** As a cricket batsman. **A.39** Wool, coal &/or opals. **A.40** The inclusion of Aborigines on the national census, allowing them to vote.

Society & culture,
then and now

Above: Most Australians are fiercely patriotic.

Above: In 2008, the Australian government's apology to Aboriginal people who had been removed from their families under previous policies of assimilation, was a step towards reconciliation between Aborigines and white Australians.

Life for Australians is undoubtedly much easier than it was in the 1800s and 1900s, but it appears that many of the core values of Australians have changed little since those days.

AUSTRALIANS still admire honesty and loyalty in friendship and business, and exhibit a sardonic disregard for authority or bureaucracy. They still respect hard workers and bosses who "chip in". Australians also believe in the freedom of speech, religion, vote and choice.

GREAT AUSTRALIAN DREAM

The desire to own or control land, both for white Australians and Aborigines, is an ongoing thread that runs through Australian settlement history. Little has changed today. The Great Australian Dream is still to own a home and the Australian government has implemented measures, such as the first homeowners grant, to help Australians achieve their goals. Aborigines, too, are now able to take ownership of their traditional lands and many are working alongside white Australians to increase the standards of living in Aboriginal communities, which, unfortunately, remain much lower than those of white Australians. It is hoped that, by working together, we can bridge the health divide between white and black.

Right: Australia remains a relaxed and friendly place where hard work is balanced with leisure time, and sun, surf and sand are regular and relaxing pastimes.

A "FAIR GO" FOR ALL

Australia's citizens and cultural influences have been drawn from so many countries and peoples, all of whom have grasped the opportunities Australia has offered them. This has meant that Australians do not care very much for a person's social standing by birth or background and tend to judge people by who they are, not by where they were born, what school they attended or who their parents were. Australians are also supportive of "battlers" and underdogs, those who struggle to "improve their lot" and make a better life for themselves. Equal opportunity for all — the celebrated "fair go" — means that no-one should be discriminated against due to sex, colour, race, country of birth, political or sexual preference, or religion. Federal laws to protect these freedoms mean that Australia is truly a lucky country.

the FACTS!

AUTHOR SIR WALTER MURDOCH called the typical Australian of the 1930s "humorous, inarticulate, sagacious, easy going, loyal to his own ethical code" — a reputation Aussies still own today.

AUSTRALIANS still live much of their lives outdoors and most enjoy camping and "going bush". Enjoying a barbecue outside (below) or dining al fresco remain popular.

WOMEN HAD TO WEAR at least 7.5 cm of fabric at the hip of their bikinis or they could be arrested in the 1960s. Now, Australian women are free to wear what they like, whether bikini or burkha, provided they are not exposing themselves in public.

TODAY'S "BRONZED AUSSIES" are aware that the country has the highest rate of skin cancer in the world and know to slip, slop, slap (slip on a shirt, slop on sunscreen and slap on a hat).

TOLERANCE, RESPECT, a sense of humour in adversity and a willingness to lend a hand to those in need are typical Aussie qualities.

Further reading

PUBLICATIONS

Angus & Robertson Concise Australian Encyclopedia, Revised Edition, Angus & Robertson, North Ryde, 1986

Barwick, J. & J. *Australian History in the 20th Century*, Heinemann Library, Reed Educational & Professional Publishing, Port Melbourne, 2000

Burke, E. & Mirams, S. *Australian History: Dreamtime to the Great War*, Oxford University Press, South Melbourne, 2001

Child, M. *Australia's Second Century 1901–present*, Murray David Publishing, Newtown, 2004

Clark, M., Hoopers, M. & Ferrier, S. *History of Australia*, Scholastic, Gosford, 1995

Cox, K. *Amazing Facts About Australia's Early Explorers*, Steve Parish Publishing, Brisbane, 2008

Cox, K. *Amazing Facts About Australia's Early Settlers*, Steve Parish Publishing, Brisbane, 2009

Cox, K. *Wildflowers of Western Australia*, Steve Parish, Publishing, Brisbane, 2006

Fraser, B. (Ed) *The Macquarie Encyclopedia of Australian Events*, The Macquarie Library, Macquarie University, 1997

Jones, C. *A Time Machine Through Australia 1788–1901: Back to Adelaide*, Macmillan Library, South Yarra, Victoria, 2004

Jones, C. *A Time Machine Through Australia 1788–1901: Back to Port Phillip*, Macmillan Education Australia, South Yarra, Victoria, 2004

Jones, C. *A Time Machine Through Australia 1788–1901: Back to Sydney Cove*, Macmillan Education Australia, South Yarra, Victoria, 2004

Jones, C. *A Time Machine Through Australia 1788–1901; Back to Swan River*, Macmillan Education, South Yarra, Victoria, 2004

Laws, J. & Stewart, C. *It Doesn't End There*, Pan Macmillan, Sydney, 2006

Laws, J. & Stewart, C. *There's Always More to the Story*, Pan Macmillan Australia, Sydney 2004

Luck, P. *This Fabulous Century*, New Holland Publishing, Frenchs Forest, 1999

Nicholson, M. *The Little Aussie Fact Book*, Penguin Books, Camberwell, Vic, 2002

Random House Australia, *Australia Through Time*, Random House, Milsons Point, 2001

Reader's Digest Book of Australian Facts, Reader's Digest (Australia) Pty Ltd, Surry Hills, 1992

WEBSITES

www.trove.nla.gov.au
www.abc.net.au/queensland/heritage
www.environment.gov.au/heritage
www.fedsquare.com
www.gutenberg.net.au
www.museumvictoria.com.au
www.norfolkisland.com.au

AKUBRA ® A type of traditional "slouch" hat made of rabbit pelt and worn by Australian bushmen, the Australian Infantry and Aussies in general.

ANCESTOR Someone a person is descended from, usually distantly — a forefather.

ANZAC A member of the Australian and New Zealand Army Corps serving in World War I.

AUSTRALIA FELIX Thomas Mitchell coined this term when he discovered lush pasture in Victoria. *Felix* is Latin for "happy" or "blessed".

BILLABONG A waterhole that runs only during the wet season.

BILLY A metal pot or kettle used for boiling water or making tea.

BLOKE An Australian male.

BOUNDARY RIDER A station hand who maintains the property's fences to prevent stock from straying.

BUSHRANGER A bandit or outlaw in colonial times, often hiding out in the bush.

CANNIBAL An animal or person that eats others of its own species.

CONTINENT One of the main land masses of the world (there are seven).

DIGGER An Australian or New Zealand solider serving in the army.

DREAMING Aboriginal spiritual beliefs that include the past, present and future and describe the relationship between people, spirits, plants, animals and objects.

DROVER Someone who herds sheep or cattle, usually over long distances.

EMIGRANT A person who is leaving their own country to go and live in another.

ENDEMIC Found in a particular location and nowhere else.

EVOLVE To change through descending generations.

EXTINCT Having no living examples of the same kind, or species.

FEDERATION When the States of Australia decided to join together to form a national framework for government, law and defence.

FOSSIL Remains or traces of a once-living organism.

GENUS (PLURAL: GENERA) A group of one or more closely related species. The first Latin name of a living organism's scientific name is the genus. Different species can share the same genus.

HABITAT Where an animal/plant lives.

IMMIGRANT A person who has come from another country to live in Australia.

INVERTEBRATE An animal that does not have a backbone.

JACKEROO A young man working on a farm.

JILLAROO A young woman working on a farm.

KIWI A friendly Australian nickname for New Zealanders.

LARRIKIN A mischievous, but good-natured person.

LARVA (PLURAL: LARVAE) Any immature animal e.g. tadpoles.

MAMMAL A class of vertebrates that share features such as being covered in hair and feeding young on milk produced by the mother.

MARSUPIALS Mammals that carry their young in a pouch.

MEMBRANE A thin, pliable sheet or layer of animal tissue.

MONOTREME An unusual egg-laying mammal that has only one hole for reproductive and waste purposes.

OPAL A gemstone formed from a mineral. Opals can take many colours, including opalescent, green, blue, magenta or orange.

PREDATOR An animal that hunts and eats other animals.

SPAWN The eggs and sperm of frogs, fish and aquatic invertebrates. Also the act of laying eggs for these animals.

SPECIES A group of animals that can breed together to produce fertile offspring.

SWAG Waterproof bedding that, when rolled up, can carry personal belongings.

THONGS Rubber, uncovered shoes that are held on the foot by a band between the big toe and other toes.

TOXIC Poisonous.

VERTEBRATE Animal with a backbone surrounding the spinal cord and a skull protecting the brain.

Index